VICTORY
ROAD

VICTORY ROAD

The Ride of My Life

HELIO CASTRONEVES

WITH **Marissa Matteo**

A CELEBRA BOOK

Celebra
Published by New American Library, a division of
Penguin Group (USA) Inc., 375 Hudson Street,
New York, New York 10014, USA
Penguin Group (Canada), 90 Eglinton Avenue East, Suite 700, Toronto,
Ontario M4P 2Y3, Canada (a division of Pearson Penguin Canada Inc.)
Penguin Books Ltd., 80 Strand, London WC2R 0RL, England
Penguin Ireland, 25 St. Stephen's Green, Dublin 2,
Ireland (a division of Penguin Books Ltd.)
Penguin Group (Australia), 250 Camberwell Road, Camberwell, Victoria 3124,
Australia (a division of Pearson Australia Group Pty. Ltd.)
Penguin Books India Pvt. Ltd., 11 Community Centre, Panchsheel Park,
New Delhi - 110 017, India
Penguin Group (NZ), 67 Apollo Drive, Rosedale, North Shore 0632,
New Zealand (a division of Pearson New Zealand Ltd.)
Penguin Books (South Africa) (Pty.) Ltd., 24 Sturdee Avenue,
Rosebank, Johannesburg 2196, South Africa

Penguin Books Ltd., Registered Offices:
80 Strand, London WC2R 0RL, England

Published by Celebra, an imprint of New American Library,
a division of Penguin Group (USA) Inc.

First Printing, June 2010
10 9 8 7 6 5 4 3 2 1

Copyright © Castroneves Publishing, LLC, 2010
Foreword copyright © Roger Penske, 2010
All rights reserved

Text photo credits are on page 285.

CELEBRA and logo are trademarks of Penguin Group (USA) Inc.

LIBRARY OF CONGRESS CATALOGING-IN-PUBLICATION DATA:
Castroneves, Helio.
  Victory road: the ride of my life/Helio Castroneves with Marissa Matteo.
    p. cm.
  ISBN 978-0-451-22737-9
  1. Castroneves, Helio. 2. Automobile racing drivers—Brazil—Biography.
I. Matteo, Marissa. II. Title.
  GV1032.C38A3 2010
  796.72092—dc22
  [B]   2010009186

Set in ITC New Baskerville
Designed by Pauline Neuwirth

Printed in the United States of America

Without limiting the rights under copyright reserved above, no part of this publication may be
reproduced, stored in or introduced into a retrieval system, or transmitted, in any form, or by
any means (electronic, mechanical, photocopying, recording, or otherwise), without the prior
written permission of both the copyright owner and the above publisher of this book.

PUBLISHER'S NOTE
Publisher does not have any control over and does not assume any responsibility for author
or third-party Web sites or their content.

The scanning, uploading, and distribution of this book via the Internet or via any other means
without the permission of the publisher is illegal and punishable by law. Please purchase
only authorized electronic editions, and do not participate in or encourage electronic piracy
of copyrighted materials. Your support of the author's rights is appreciated.

To Luke Weber, whose optimism reminds me that it is enough to simply have the opportunity every day to pursue your dreams.

To Kati, who I first thought gave up her dreams so I could pursue mine. Only now I realize that attaining my dream was actually her dream, too.

To my parents, whose dream was that my sister and I would love and support each other along the way. That dream has come true.

And to Adriana and Mikaella, for whom I will work very hard to help make their dreams come true.

Contents

Foreword   ix

Introduction   xiii

Part 1: *Ladies and Gentlemen, Start Your Engines*

    CHAPTER 1: *Stop*   7

    CHAPTER 2: *Driven*   23

    CHAPTER 3: *Testing*   63

    CHAPTER 4: *Slow Down*   81

    CHAPTER 5: *Summoned to the Pits*   97

Part 2

    CHAPTER 6: *180 Degrees*   115

    CHAPTER 7 *My First Indy*   129

    CHAPTER 8: *Chasing History*   145

    CHAPTER 9: *On Trial*   157

    CHAPTER 10: *Quickstepping*   171

Part 3

CHAPTER 11: *Stop, Slow Down, Go Back*   199

CHAPTER 12: *Losing Control*   211

CHAPTER 13: *Preparation*   223

CHAPTER 14: *A Time of Trial*   235

CHAPTER 15: *Closing In*   253

CHAPTER 16: *Back on Track*   265

CONCLUSION: *The Beginning*   271

Appendix   277

Acknowledgments   281

Foreword

E VEN BEFORE HELIO joined Team Penske, I had been
watching him at the tracks. When the helmet was off,
he was all smiles; when the helmet was on, he was all business. He was just the kind of guy you wanted to root for and
the kind of driver you wanted on your team. So I was excited
when he came on board in 2000. He immediately fit into the
team culture, but he also brought something refreshing and
uniquely Helio. It became apparent that we had signed not
just a great driver, but also a great character, which he revealed
to the fans during one of his first races of that season.

We were at the Detroit Grand Prix on Belle Isle, where Helio
captured his first CART (Championship Auto Racing Teams)
win. When he crossed the line, I knew that it would be the first
of many impressive victories. However, I did not expect what
would happen next. Helio stopped the car at the finish line, ran
to the fence, and started to climb. I had never seen anything like
it. Nobody had. The crowd went wild. It was a thrilling sight to
watch our new, young driver hanging from the fence, eager to
share his joy with the fans. You could not help but be caught up
in the moment. His excitement was contagious.

With that first fence climb, Helio brought something new
to our sport—an enthusiasm and energy that the fans had
been looking for all along. They started calling him Spider-
Man and chanting the nickname as soon as he entered the

tracks. Young boys wore Spider-Man costumes in the stands. He became an overnight fan favorite. In that first season, he climbed the fence three times and earned three pole positions. He established himself as not just a fun guy to watch, but also a world-class driver.

For all of the passion and fervor Helio displays after he crosses the line, when he is in the car he is one of the most tenacious and focused drivers I have ever seen. This was never more apparent than when Helio raced in his first Indianapolis 500-mile race. It was 2001 and our team was returning to the Brickyard for the first time in five years. Indianapolis is a difficult track, but Helio was determined and unwavering in his preparation. For the month building up to the 500, he was working, listening and building up his confidence. On race day, he was raring to go—and he did not disappoint. In the final laps, he edged out his teammate, Gil de Ferran, and we finished first and second for the first time in our team's history. Helio made his first Indy fence climb, and it was exhilarating to watch the massive crowd chant his name as he pumped his fist in celebration.

When we returned to the Brickyard in 2002, there was much speculation about whether Helio could become the first driver in thirty years to win back-to-back Indys. I promised Helio that if he accomplished the impressive feat, I would climb the fence with him. Helio, true to form, remained calm and purposeful as soon as he put the helmet on. It was a close and controversial race, but he delivered another exciting victory. And I took my first fence climb.

Helio is the first (and quite possibly the only) driver who could inspire me to scale the fence at the Brickyard. Of course, he continued his climb as he captured his third Indianapolis 500 victory in 2009, becoming one of only nine drivers in history to earn three wins at Indy.

Helio's passion and fun-loving personality are infectious. When he is around, you cannot help but get caught up in his story. And he has written himself a great story.

I look forward to watching the future chapters unfold.

—*Roger Penske*

Introduction

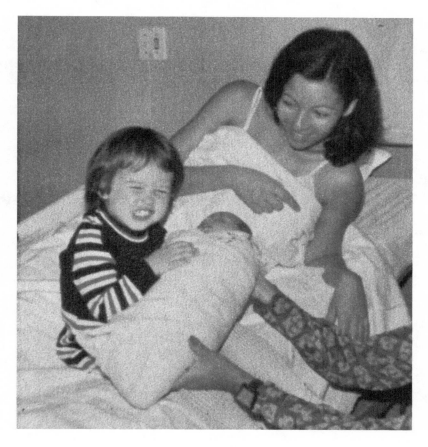

I WAS BORN IN São Paulo, Brazil, on May 10, 1975, and grew up in a town called Ribeirão Preto. I was raised by Helio Castro Neves Sr., a man who loved racing, and Sandra Castro Neves, a woman who loathed it.

My father is smart, loving, and always in a good mood. Yet he has also been a fighter when he needs to be (that is, every time my mother tried to get him to stop my racing). All my life I have tried to live by his example and his philosophy: *To be a champion, you must act like a champion.*

My mother is a sweet, elegant, and religious woman. In my early days of racing she would stand on the sidelines with her rosary, praying for me to stay in the back of the pack so I wouldn't get hurt (she still grips the rosary, but no longer prays for me to be in the back). She tried as hard as she could to get me to pursue anything but racing—something stable and safe—but eventually, she let go. She had faith in the words she repeated to me over and over again: *God has a plan.*

My sister, Kati, and I were brought up to live by these duel philosophies: "Act like a champion" and "God has a plan." We were also taught to stick together. Life is a team effort. I've always known that if I just turned around, Kati would be there with her brown eyes twinkling, a huge smile across her face. I began racing in 1987, and though my mother dragged her to the first few races, Kati soon became my biggest (and loudest) cheerleader. In return, I was dragged to her ballet recitals (which I never fully enjoyed until I was about thirteen and fully able to appreciate the wonder of twenty girls in spandex).

In the fall of 2007, I was more readily able to understand what it takes to be a dancer when I appeared on the hit TV show *Dancing with the Stars.* Kati flew from Miami to Los Angeles every week to see me. "It's not so easy, huh?" she would say. And I had to agree. But I was in it to win it. I refused to go home without that trophy, which now takes a prominent place in my home among my most important motor racing trophies.

Everything was great. I had an extremely successful career racing cars on the IndyCar circuit and I was a two-time winner of the most important open-wheel race in the world, the Indy 500. I lived in a beautiful house in South Florida; I was a young man having a good time planning how I could reach my next professional goal of winning the IndyCar championship after coming so close so many times, including the 2008 season.

Then, in October 2008, Kati and I were indicted on six counts of tax evasion. My life collapsed around me. The big house, the fancy cars, the trophies, and Indy rings all became symbols of a past time. In one day, I went from a racetrack to a jail cell. In one day, my world shifted forever.

A few months before I was indicted, I started dating Adriana, a dark-haired, dark-eyed Colombian beauty. We met at the baggage claim in the Cartagena airport; we had been on the same flight from Miami and the moment I saw her, I was captivated. Not only was she beautiful, but she exuded confidence and a cool sense of calm.

Adriana and I started dating in January 2008 and the indictment came in October of the same year. I was sure that when I told her about the case, she was going to flee. Instead, she stood, solid as a rock, right by my side. She is one of the strongest women I have ever met and she challenges me to be a better person. On one of our first dates, I was nervous and I guess I was talking a little too much (which is very unlike me!). She looked at me and waited until I shut up. Then she said, "You are the master of your thoughts and the slave of what you say." I was both impressed and even more enamored. I knew right then that she was different from any woman I had ever met.

Today, Adriana is the mother of our child. I am proud (and a little scared) to say that our daughter, Mikaella, seems to be taking on the same strong personality as her mother. Man, I have a long road ahead of me.

There is another philosophy that I live by: *Tomorrow is another day.* There are many ways of looking at racing cars that can be transferred to everyday life. You have to take each race as it comes. You can only win the race you are driving so take each day as it comes. That means that every challenge should be met in its own time. I view all of life as one long race. Neither the long race nor the individual races that make it up are going to be won on the first lap. That's one of the first things you learn as a race car driver. You have to pace yourself, and hang in there when it gets a little scary. Sometimes you have to take your foot off the throttle and save fuel. Sometimes you have to go maximum speed. Although you are the one driving the car, this is a team effort—you are not alone, though it may feel like it at times. You must maintain control and always believe in yourself. And remember, if there is a problem—and there will be problems—it is because there is a solution for it.

—*Helio Castroneves*

Part I
Ladies and Gentlemen, Start Your Engines

Between the beginning and the end, there is always a middle.

—BRAZILIAN PROVERB

I T IS A warm afternoon in Indianapolis. The National Anthem plays and four hundred thousand fans have their hands over their hearts. The final words echo through the stadium: "O'er the land of the free . . . and the home of the brave . . ."

I stand with my team, my car positioned at the starting line on the Indianapolis Motor Speedway. My sister is in the pits with my parents. My father's credo echoes in my head: "To be a champion, you must act like a champion." I puff out my chest and stand a little taller (if I'm lucky I can reach a towering five feet, eight inches on my tiptoes).

The driver introductions begin.

"Starting in the thirty-third position . . ." The announcer's voice booms, and the adrenaline begins to pump through my veins. The crowd begins to hum. As the drivers' names are called I fade in and out.

Four hundred thousand people surround me; the place is brimming with excitement.

"Starting in the tenth position . . . Danica Patrick." The crowd cheers louder and I snap back to attention. There are some boos. I am surprised. Danica usually gets all the adoration. I look around the speedway. I am just as astounded by the size of the place as I was the first time I set foot in the cathedral of American racing.

I hear my childhood friend announced: "Starting in the sixth position . . . Tony Kanaan." I remember the two of us as kids in São Paulo learning how to navigate track corners and chase girls.

"Starting in second position. Ryan Briscoe." I look to my teammate standing next to me. I want to ask him if this is real. I want to make sure that I am not in a dream.

"And now for the pole position. Two-time Indy Five Hundred chaaaampion, Helio Castroneves." The entire stadium roars louder than I have ever heard before. Even with my earplugs in, it is deafening. I turn to Ryan. "Wow," I say. "That was amazing."

"Impressive, mate," he tells me.

"Drivers, to your cars."

I step into the car and whistle a song to calm me down: *In every life we have some trouble / But when you worry you make it double. / Don't worry. Be happy.*

I grab on to the steering wheel.

Focus, I tell myself. Focus.

The archbishop performs the invocation.

It's just another race. Same as every other race.

A trumpet sounds out taps.

You are not going to win it in the first lap. Pace yourself.

The marching band begins to play "Back Home Again in Indiana" and a thousand balloons are released into the sky.

Hang tough. Maintain control.

"Ladies and gentlemen, start your engines."

To be a champion, you must act like a champion.

Deus tem um plano. God has a plan.

CHAPTER 1

Stop

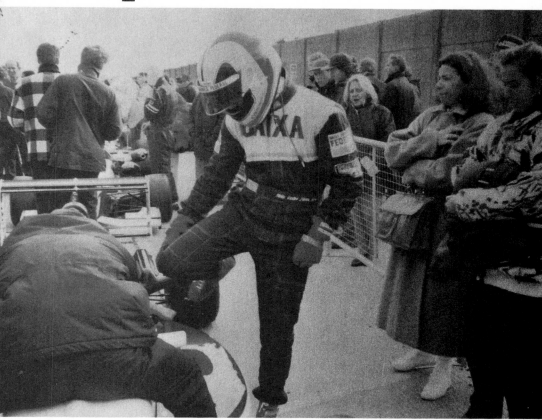

**Because in a split
second, it's gone.**
—AYRTON SENNA

A LL MY LIFE, *I've been on the hunt for a few hundredths of a second. It is all I know. My focus has always been: Look ahead, go faster, just drive. I have never been told, Stop, slow down, go back. Yet for the past six months, I have been preparing for this trial, and every day, the lawyers ask me to rewind. Tell us that story again. Try to recall the details. Stop. Slow down. Go back. Go back.*

It is agony.

I am not sleeping. I am barely eating. I should be racing, but I haven't been in a car in months.

With each passing day, as the trial preparations drag on, I slowly come to realize just how much my family and I have sacrificed in the name of my racing career—the time, the money, the years of dedication and determination. I quickly come to realize that it could all be taken from me, from us, in an instant.

Worst of all, the whole damn nightmare plays in slow motion.

It is March 3, 2009. I am sitting in a courtroom in Miami waiting for something to happen. The clerk stands up. "All rise. The Honorable Judge Donald L. Graham presiding."

A tall, stately man walks in, dressed in a black robe, with a military crew cut and a stern look on his face. He sits down and tells us, "Be seated."

We all sit back down. I feel as though I am playing a part in a movie. The judge is perfectly cast. The courtroom is cold and a bit dim. The attorneys have set their jaws in a stern and serious manner. The jury sits still and attentive. The clerk's voice rings through the courtroom, strong and clear.

"The court will now hear the case of the United States of America versus Helio Castroneves."

Holy. Shit.

The United States of America.

Versus me.

The movie begins to blur into reality and I struggle to maintain my focus. A prosecutor stands up to give his opening statement. He is talking about me and I try to pay close attention, but I get lost in his words.

I don't know much about legal proceedings, but I know this much: I know that I have been charged with six counts of tax evasion. I know that my sister and my business attorney have been charged with the same six counts and we have all been charged with conspiracy. I know that we have done nothing wrong, yet I am also aware that we could go to jail for ten years. This would mean the end of my racing career and deportation back to Brazil. And all I want is to be on a racetrack, training for the upcoming season.

My lawyer, Roy Black, walks in front of the jury box. "Now in order to understand what happened in this case, you have to understand something about Helio. As a young boy, it became obvious early on that he was supremely talented in racing. That he was born with the gift . . . "

I look down. I am not sure what to do with my eyes or my hands. I pick up my notebook and stare at a blank page.

Roy continues: ". . . that he had the reflexes, he had the hand-eye coordination, he had the ability to do things that most human beings could only dream of. And he possessed the supreme courage that it takes to participate in his sport, a sport where you drive cars at two hundred miles an hour, traveling farther than a football field in less than a second. You need reflexes, you need instincts, you need abilities beyond which most of us possess."

I look at the jury box. I scan the eyes of the ten people who will decide my fate. The prosecutor has just told them that I am a criminal. *You don't know me,* I want to tell them. *I am not a criminal. I am a good person. I love this country just like you. This country gave me opportunities. It allowed me to achieve my dream.*

I make eye contact with a juror and I immediately look away. I stare back to my notebook and begin to write out prayers.

Pai-Nosso que estais no Céu, santificado seja o Vosso nome.

Our Father, who art in Heaven, hallowed be Thy name.

I hear Roy's voice. It sounds a thousand miles away. "In order to nourish Helio's talent, his family gave up almost everything. His father had a business in which he spent almost all of his money promoting, managing, supervising, and assisting his son, Helio. His sister, Kati, who had been a ballerina, who had danced professionally, gave up her career to work with her brother. You will see this is a very close family that did everything it could to assist Helio to achieve his dream. Helio's dream became the family dream."

I keep my head down and try to hold back my tears. I don't dare look at Kati or my parents, but the words ring in my ears. "Helio's dream became the family dream."

E agora, I write, *o pesadelo de família.*

And now, the family nightmare.

How did this happen? How did I end up in this nightmare? And how did I bring my family along with me? I cannot answer these questions, but I can vividly recall the moment the dream was born.

ƒ

It is springtime in Brazil, 1981. I am five years old, hiding in the trunk of my father's car. I hear muffled voices as he drives past the track security. My father owns a stock car team, Team Corpal. He takes me along with him to every race, but in order to get into the racetracks, you must be sixteen years old. I am used to burying myself in this trunk. I feel the car driving a few more yards and then stopping. I hear the door open and the familiar sound of my father's footsteps coming for me. He opens the trunk, lifts me out, and tousles my hair, and without a word I go and sit in the car with the other guys—an engineer, two mechanics, and the driver Alfredo Guaraná Menezes. Alfredo, or "Tío Guaraná" as I call him, was one of the best Brazilian race car drivers in the 1970s. He is very tall, thin, and has long curly hair. His voice is low but firm. He is my first racing idol. He tells me stories about competing against Formula One champions like Nelson Piquet and Emerson Fittipaldi. I listen as though he is telling me the secrets to life.

When we get to pit row, I walk in between my father and Tío Guaraná so as not to be seen by the track officials. In our pit stall, my father lifts me up and hides me between two stacks of tires. "Yell if you need anything, Helinho," my father says, like anyone would hear me over the roar of the engines. I squeeze down into the corner and watch the men start to work. I inhale the perfume of gasoline and motor oil. I am comforted by the lull of engines and cars whipping around the track. Everything about the sport enchants me. I am in love.

For five years, I spend my Saturdays hiding in the trunk of my father's car and hiding in the corner of Team Corpal's pit stall. On our drives back home, I ask my father questions about the race, the car, and Tío Guaraná. I find out that Tío had been asked to race Formula One in Europe with Piquet, but instead chose to stay in Brazil. "Why?" I ask my father. He only shrugs.

In 1986, my father decides that Team Corpal will no longer compete, but the men do not let go of one another. Instead of heading to the racetracks of São Paulo on the weekends, they all meet at an abandoned track in São Carlos, seventy miles outside my hometown of Ribeirão Preto. I tag along with my father. I am happy to be included and happy to no longer have to hide in the trunk. My uncles, my grandfathers, and some of my dad's employees join us in a caravan every Saturday. They park their cars on the side of the track and set up a barbecue and a circle of lawn chairs. They take turns flipping the meat on the grill and racing the go-karts around the track.

On my eleventh birthday, Tío Guaraná gives me my first go-kart. I spend hours running it around the circuit. There is no finesse to my technique. Gas, brake, gas, brake. But I love the feeling of being in control of something. My arms start to throb with the vibration of the steering wheel, but I refuse to quit. When we drive back home that night, my father tells me, "Don't tell your mother about the go-kart. It will be our secret."

My mother despises racing. She does not want me around it, let alone behind the wheel. For weeks we don't say a word about the go-kart. As far as she is concerned, my father and I are just going to São Carlos for barbecues.

Late one Saturday afternoon, I am on the track. I've been driving all afternoon as the men sit on the side, eating and watching me go. With each turn I am gaining speed and confidence. I take a corner too hard and careen into the wall and the kart goes flipping. In an instant, my father is there. "Are you okay?" I am in only a T-shirt and shorts and I can feel the skin that has been ripped off my knees and elbows. Dad picks me up. "You're okay," he tells me. I am shaken up and I feel all parts of my body begin to throb. We go to the hospital, where they clean me up a bit. I can now clearly see the skin I have lost and the bruises beginning to form.

"What are we going to tell Mom?" I say.

"Don't worry. I'll handle it."

We leave the hospital and I think we are going back home, but instead my father takes me back to the track. "What are we doing?" I ask.

"We're going to drive." He gets into a kart and tells me to sit on his lap.

I hesitate. He smiles, letting me know that it will be okay. The rest of the men look on and I am too proud to say no. I hop onto my father's lap and we fly around the track together. My father stops the kart. "Okay, now go ahead. Go on your own." I take the first few laps slowly, but soon my nerves give way to the excitement and adrenaline once more. I have learned the first lesson of racing. Never give in to the fear.

We drive the seventy miles back home and though I have conquered my anxieties on the track, I am still worried about facing my mother. There is no hiding these scrapes and bandages. My father walks in first, cheery and confident. He calls out, "Hola, Sandra! We're home!"

I try to follow his lead. "Hi, Mama!" My voice is not as strong.

She appears from the kitchen and as soon as she sees the bandages, she rushes toward me. "Oh my God, what happened?"

My eyes grow wide as they always do when I am about to lie. "Don't lie to me, Helinho. What happened?"

My father takes over. "He was driving a go-kart and he got in a little scrape-up. No big thing."

"A go-kart! He was driving a go-kart? Are you crazy? Are you trying to kill my son?!"

My mother is a little slip of a woman. Beautiful, slim, elegant. Her golden brown hair is always in place; her clothes are always in style. She is a former schoolteacher and has remained both proper and practical. Mom is disarmingly sweet, but she can turn stubborn and stern in a heartbeat. Her soft brown eyes will sharpen, her jaw will set, and you know that she means business. Like right now. Her hands are on her hips and she is staring down my father. "You are going to kill my son," she tells Dad.

My father is a teddy bear of a man, short and a bit pudgy, always smiling and always in a good mood. He has these blue twinkling eyes that reveal his childlike optimism. His whole face naturally falls into a smile, making it impossible to stay mad at him. "Sandra, it's no big deal. He's fine. Look at him. He's fine."

"He is not fine! Look at these bandages!"

"Boys get scraped up. It happens."

"Go wash up," my mother tells me. "It's time for dinner."

As I walk up the stairs, I hear the argument continue and my mother's final words as she walks away: "That is the first and last time he ever sets foot in a go-kart. Do you hear me?"

I am certain that my racing days are over, but the next weekend, my father calls to me, "Helinho, are you coming?"

"Coming where?"

"To the track. We are all waiting for you." The men are all standing by their cars, with packed coolers and cases of beer, just like every other Saturday. I look to my mother. Her arms are crossed and her jaw is set, but she gives me a brief nod to tell me it is okay. I don't know what my father has said to her, but I do know that she is not going to give up so easily.

Each Saturday, the men continue to take me to São Carlos.

My mother puts up a futile counterattack. She enrolls me in swimming, judo, soccer, volleyball, tennis—anything possible to keep me away from the track. I try each sport for a few days, maybe a week—long enough for Mom to buy the uniform and all the equipment—and then I tell her I want to quit. It is too late. She knows it. I know it. My father knows it. He has won. The racing has already entered my bloodstream.

Weekend after weekend, I continue to drive around the track, but I begin to grow bored of racing against myself. "Dad, are there any other kids who can drive go-karts? Or am I the only one?"

He laughs. "Of course there are." But how am I to know? We live in a small farming town a hundred fifty miles from São Paulo. I've never seen another kid in a go-kart.

One night, in the spring of 1987, my father comes into my room with a stack of papers. "Look what I have for you," he says. Oh no, I think, I must have failed a test at school. When he shows me the papers, I see that it is an application.

"I've enrolled you in the Karting State Championships," he says.

The state championships? I have never even seen another kid in a go-kart.

The following weekend, Dad, Mom, Kati, and I drive to São Paulo. Kati and my mother are not happy about it. My mother is upset that she lost the battle. Kati is upset that she is missing a party. My father is thrilled. I am terrified.

When we walk into the stadium, I see hundreds and hundreds of go-karts. My legs start to quiver. I look to the ground and see black marks all around the track left by the tires from other go-karts. "These mark the several options of routes around the circuit," my father tells me. I have no idea what he means.

My fear must be apparent, because my mother leans over and whispers to me, "If you don't want to do it, you don't have to. We can go back home."

I look to my dad and see how excited he is. "No, no," I tell my mom. "I want to!"

I walk to the pits with Dad, while Mom and Kati go to sit in the stands. "Are you ready?" Dad asks. I nod. I am nervous and excited. Mostly nervous. I put on my helmet, buckle into my go-kart, and head out of the pits. Right away, I make my first big rookie mistake—instead of coming out of the pit exit, I come out of the entrance. I immediately flip myself around. I drive one lap, then stop. The noise from all of the go-karts intimidates me. "Why are you stopping?" Dad calls out. "Keep going! Keep going!"

I begin to drive again, following the other go-karts, and I start to get the hang of it. The experience on this São Paulo track is completely different from driving alone in São Carlos. It takes a while to get used to the added noise, the added go-karts, and the added excitement. But by the end of the day, I am both comfortable and energized. I have caught the bug. "When are we coming back to this track?" I ask my dad.

Dad begins to take me to the São Paulo track every other weekend, pulling me out of school on Thursday afternoons; we stay at a hotel. My mother is not happy that I am missing so much school. She insists that if I don't maintain my grades, she will pull me out of racing. My father arranges it with my teachers so that I can take all of my tests early in the week, and I make sure to do well—or well enough to pass, anyway. I will do anything to keep racing.

In São Paulo, I train with about twenty other drivers my age, among them Tony Kanaan, Felipe Giaffone, Bruno Junquera, Rodrigo Casarini, and Enrique Bernouldi. They call me Caipira (the Hillbilly) or Pé Vermelho (the Red Foot), because of the red dirt in Ribeirão Preto. I make a point to prove to them that even though I am a Red Foot, I am a good Red Foot.

The twenty of us become fast friends, running through the São Paulo hotels, going to the arcades, and spending hours together at the track. Our track days begin at ten in the morning and last until five or six at night. At noon we break for lunch, and after we eat we organize impromptu soccer matches. We play in our racing suits, with the top halves tied around our waists. Our fathers stand on the sidelines, telling each other how their sons are sure to be the next big racing superstars. We boys do not concern ourselves with such discussions. We are not yet old enough to see each other as enemies or opponents. We are friends. We are having fun. For now.

For the first race of the 1987 season, my whole family comes to watch: Mom, Kati, grandparents, aunts, uncles, cousins, dogs. The men are excited, roaring in the stands. The women are nervous, gripping their rosaries. During the qualifying round, I start off strong and fast, but then I spin out and end up in the back of the pack. When I see my mother, she hugs me. "Great job!"

I hear my grandmother whisper to her, "Oh thank God. As long as he is in the back, he can't get hurt!"

In the race, I finish twelfth out of thirty—not bad, but still not good. I want a trophy and only the top six get trophies. Dad and I drive home together and talk about the race. "It's a very good start," he tells me. "Next week you'll do better."

He is right. The next week I qualify in the top row and place in the top ten. But still, no trophy. The men grow more excited. The women are still leery of the sport. My mother continually tells me, "Whenever you want to stop, just tell me, okay? If you are not enjoying this, you can stop." But we both know that is not going to happen. I am having too much fun. And that is what these early days of racing are about—fun.

I love going to São Paulo, spending the weekends in the city, and spending time with my father. I love having twenty new friends from all corners of Brazil and of course, I love the racing. It is much like the early days of any sport. There is no pressure, no expectation, no overthinking. When you begin playing soccer, it is a game of kick and run, kick and run. Later you learn to pass, to anticipate the play, to judge the field. It is the same in racing. At first it is a sport of accelerate and brake, accelerate and brake. As the days go on, you learn to ease into the turns, to wait for the right moment to pass, to use the pedals with some finesse. And once you start to acquire a few of these skills, you learn about competition.

During one of the first qualifying rounds, I am running in the front of the pack. I have been in the front of the pack most of the races, but my friend, Casarini, has been struggling in the back. Going into one of the final turns, I see that he is close behind me. I let him pass me on the corner so that he can have a strong finish.

"Hey, what was that?" my mother asks me when the qualifier ends. "Why did you let Casarini pass you?"

"He is my friend," I say. "I wanted him to do well, too."

She shakes her rosary at me. "This is not a game. This is a contest. You have to fight for it out there."

I look at her, but do not say anything.

She immediately tries to take it back. She speaks softer. "I'm sorry. You know what? This is about having fun. I'm sorry. I'm sorry." But she knows and I know that this is a turning point. We have entered a corner and for the rest of the season, I am learning to navigate this turn.

Mom and Kati are there for every race and I can tell they no longer dread it; they actually quite enjoy it. And they become just as competitive as anyone else; especially Kati. She learns all of the rules and regulations. Each race she brings a cheering section of her friends and they sit in the stands with my grandparents, aunts, uncles, and cousins. Weekends at the racetrack have become a family affair.

During the week, Dad and I begin to go to São Paulo more often for practice sessions. As I acquire more technique and skill, I begin to climb my way up in the standings. Midway through the year, I win my first trophy, for fourth place in a field of over one hundred go-karts. I cannot wait to get back to Ribeirão Preto to show my friends and my grandfather. My friends tell me, "But it's only fourth place."

"I know. Don't worry; I'll get better."

My grandfather's reaction is much more gratifying. He takes the trophy in his hands, holds it up, and looks at me. In a thoughtful, serious tone, he tells me, "Helio, this is going to be the first of many."

The final weekend of the season, it is pouring rain. The go-karts are slipping all over the track. I feel the wheels skidding under me each time I brake into a turn. I wonder what would happen if I brake a little later and use the rim of the track to slow me down instead of my brakes. On the next corner, I try it, flying into the track rim and turning the wheel as I do. I do not skid, I do not slow down, and I come out of the corner three car lengths ahead of the other guys. I decide that I like racing in the rain and the rest of the afternoon I go careening from corner to corner, pleased with my new discovery. When I go to the side where all of the fathers are standing, I can tell that I have done something impressive. They all congratulate me and my father cannot hide his pride. "That was amazing, Helinho. Really amazing!"

I recognize that I have turned another important corner in my racing career. A few nights later, my parents, Kati, and I are sitting down to dinner. Halfway through the meal, Dad tells my mother, "I have sold the property in Rio."

My mother balks. "What do you mean, you sold the property? For what reason?"

"I am using the money to start a go-kart team for Helinho. And to hire him a publicist."

"Are you crazy? This is not smart."

"Sandra, he has the God-given talent."

"But how do you know?" My mother wants some assurance that the money is not being frittered away. "How can you be sure?"

"I just know. It's in his reflexes. The way he turns the corners. There is no fear. The other men all know it, too. I hear them talk."

"And why would he need a publicist? He is only fourteen."

"Because this is how it is done, Sandra. You hire a publicist and get his name in the press. He needs exposure in order to get sponsorships in the future. This is just the beginning."

Nobody speaks for a moment. And then my father says something I'll never forget. "He's got the gift." These are the words that matter to me. Not that my father has sold his property or that I am getting a publicist. No, it is because my father tells Kati and my mother (and I suppose himself), "He's got the gift. We're going to make him the greatest driver of all time."

I am fourteen and this is all I hear.

ʃ

I lift my head, a thirty-five-year-old man, forced to relive his past in this courtroom in Miami. A thirty-five-year-old man with no control over his future.

I look to Kati. She is bowing her head; her brown hair covers her face—usually a bright, happy, and smiling face, but I am sure right now she is hiding the fear that she never wants to show.

I look to my parents. Both of them appear as though they have aged ten years in the past few months. I see gray hairs and wrinkles where once there were none. I see lines marking their pain and panic.

22

How did we end up here?

I look down and scribble another prayer in my notebook.

Ave Maria, cheia de graca . . .

As I pray, I realize something before any verdict has been rendered. A realization that changes my whole outlook on life: Long ago, on a racetrack in Brazil, my dream became my family's dream. Win or lose, they believed in me every step of the way. Their support and faith is what has always driven me to win. I cannot let them down now. This is a race I cannot lose.

CHAPTER 2

Driven

**You can always go back
if you look forward.
You cannot do the reverse.**

—HELIO CASTRO NEVES, SR.

I N BRAZIL, RACING is second only to soccer. Every young boy dreams of being the next Pelé or the next Ayrton Senna. And often, when the ambition is not realized, it is passed down from father to son. I inherit my dream from my father, Helio Castro Neves Sr. It becomes our common bond. His support means everything. Without a father's backing, both financial and emotional, the goal of becoming a top driver is near impossible. In order to understand my story, or any race car driver's story, you have to know that racing is a sport that makes you pay to play. In soccer, all you need is a ball and a hell of a lot of talent. In racing, you need talent and a hell of a lot of money.

You have to pay for the car, the mechanics, the engineer, practice fees, busted engines, hotels, transportation—and on it goes. It costs hundreds of thousands of dollars, sometimes millions, to get to the level where somebody finally pays you. Often drivers never get to the top level before the money runs out. It is a common story in Brazil. A family puts all of their resources into a talented boy's racing career. Every last bit of money, time, and dedication is spent in hopes of making the boy "the greatest driver of all time." Yet all too often, the family ends up bankrupt. My story is no different.

⌒

I am thirteen years old when my father begins to pull me out of school on Wednesday afternoons. We drive the hundred fifty miles to São Paulo, where I stay until Sunday, spending my waking moments at the track. I practice Thursday and Friday, qualify on Saturday, and race on Sunday. Then we drive back to Ribeirão Preto so I can go to school on Monday and Tuesday. This does not go over without a fight from my mother.

"He needs to be in school. This is ridiculous!"

"He goes to school, Sandra. On Monday through Wednesday he goes."

"And Thursday and Friday? He spends more time at a racetrack than he does in a classroom. What happens when he stops racing?"

"Sandra, he is not going to stop racing." My father stays calm, which makes my mother even crazier.

"How do you know? He is still a child! He could decide tomorrow he doesn't want to do it anymore!"

"That is not going to happen."

She is not listening to him. She keeps going. "Then what? What kind of future is he going to have? A boy with no education?"

"Racing is his future, Sandra."

"How do you know? You have to give me a reason, some assurance."

"I just know."

"That is not enough! You need to give me something concrete!"

"I have faith."

My father knows the word that will make her stop. She will not tell him that faith is not enough.

They face each other in a silent standoff.

Neither of them says a word for at least a minute. Then my mother throws up her hands and walks out the front door. We all know where she is going. To the church, to talk to the priest or God or somebody who will take her side. We also know that this will not be the last fight.

Dad and I get in the car for the drive to São Paulo. When we start out, we talk of race strategy and technique. We talk about recent Formula One races and our three favorite drivers—Nelson Piquet, Ayrton Senna, and Emerson Fittipaldi, all Brazilians. I learn things about my father on these drives. I learn that he always dreamed of being a race car driver but his family didn't have the money; that his father died when he was ten years old and after that, his mother struggled to pay the bills; that this made him determined to succeed, determined to never be poor again.

My father explains to me why he moved our family to Ribeirão Preto in 1977 and started his company, Corpal Piping. "A year or two after you were born, the ethanol boom was beginning in Brazil. The government was encouraging farmers to grow sugarcane in order to make the ethanol. I knew that all the new sugarcane mills would need industrial piping, so I moved the family to Ribeirão Preto and started Corpal."

I stare out the window at all the farms and sugarcane mills as my father continues to talk.

"Ribeirão Preto became the largest alcohol and sugar producer in the world, and because Corpal was the only industrial pipe reseller in the region, the company became quite successful."

I am impressed. For the first time I see my father as a man and not just my dad. He tells me his dreams of making Corpal a big corporation—he is going to develop it into a brand, start a cattle feed company, create a chain of gas stations, and of course, run a racing team.

We fall silent for a long stretch of road and I stare out the window as the miles of sugarcane stalks fly past. I am thinking about racing, eager to get back on the track. When the farmland gives way to the lights of the city, I come alive.

This year, my father has hired three mechanics to work with me—Rubão, Mane, and Mario Sergio, who prepares the engine. In later years, Tato and Passoca join the team. When we get to the track, they are already working on my go-kart. I lean over the engine with them, and study each part as they open it up. Even at this very first stage, I understand that much depends on the equipment. "Racing is thirty percent driver and seventy percent car," Rubão tells me. "An average driver with an amazing car will beat an amazing driver with a crappy car every time." It is an equation I understand; it means that I should know everything about the car. The more I know, the better I will be able to communicate to Rubão and Mane about what can be done to make the cart go faster. The better I am able to communicate, the more efficiently they can work.

So it is not that I do not go to school Wednesday through Friday—it is just that I am in a different kind of school. My classroom is the São Paulo racetrack, and my teachers are Rubão, Mario, Mane, and my father. I study car engines, track aerodynamics, tire pressure, and navigating corners at different geometric angles. I begin to speak car and track lingo just as well as my father can. I understand how each part of the car works and why it is important.

I also understand that money matters. "If you want to be the best, you have to buy the best," my father tells me. And the best, of course, never comes cheap. And it is not just about the go-kart. It is the racing suit, the helmet, and the gloves. Every practice, every crash, every engine replacement, and every minor mechanical failure costs more money. Add to that travel expenses, mechanic fees, and gasoline costs and the expenses start to get pretty steep. But I do not have to worry about that. My father is willing to spend the money—he is a man on a mission. And I am happy to just drive—I am a boy living a dream.

This is the season I begin to break out. I am finishing in the top group in every race and my collection of trophies grows. With each win, my father grows more excited and more certain of his investment. He proudly displays each trophy in the dining room china case, continually shuffling around the good china. We go to the practice tracks more often; he hires another mechanic and buys me a better go-kart. We paint the "Corpal" company logo across the side of my car and as I start to earn a name for myself in the Brazilian go-kart circuits. I hear other drivers calling to me, "Hey, Corpal!" I love the feeling of recognition. And I see that my father loves it, too.

Dad and I become comrades, both on and off the track. We spend hours together in the car, traveling from city to city. We share stories and secrets. We do not tell my mother if I get hurt, or how much things cost, or if I need to leave school earlier than usual. It is not that we lie—she just never asks. She has given up the fight. She and Kati come to the races on the weekends. Mom grips her rosary and prays. Everything else she leaves to my father.

Like a lot of sports, racing can become the basis of a strong father-son relationship. Every week, from Wednesday through Sunday there are as many fathers on the track as there are young drivers. Each dad has a different parenting and coaching style. Some are screamers; some are silent observers. Some are uptight; some are laid-back. My father seems to me to be the perfect combination. He is both a coach and a cheerleader. Instead of him screaming at me if I have made a bad move, we talk it through. "You don't have to win in the first lap," he reminds me. "Wait for the

right moment to make your move. It will come. Be patient."
He is firm and honest, but he always stays positive. Because
of this, I grow to trust him and turn to him for advice and
encouragement. During the races, I look for him on the side
and he is always there. I am impatient by nature and I always
want to be in front from the first lap—Dad continually tries
to break me of the habit. Often he holds his index fingers
up to temples, a signal meaning, "Stay focused. Use your
head. You don't have to win it in the first lap."

When it is race time, nobody is more competitive than my
father. But all other times he is affable and jolly. I know that
he wants me to win, but I also know that he wants to make
sure I am having fun. He manages to be friends with everyone—the mechanics, the track officials, the other fathers,
coaches, and drivers. I learn from his example. He tells me,
"On the track you are rivals. But off the track you can still
be friends."

One afternoon I see my father talking to Tony Kanaan, a
driver in the series above me. Neither of them is smiling or
laughing and it catches my attention, because my father is
always smiling and laughing. I can tell that this is a serious
discussion.

"What were you talking to Tony about?" I ask my father
that evening.

"His father passed away last week. I was trying to comfort
him. I told him about when I lost my dad."

"Oh," I say, and then become silent. I struggle to imagine
what it must feel like to lose your father. But it is a concept
too foreign and too frightening for me to comprehend, especially as a thirteen-year-old boy. The following day, my father
calls me over and introduces me to Tony. Tony is only a year
older than me, but he looks about eighteen. He has a full
face of stubble, while I still have beanpole arms and baby-

faced skin. He is a city guy, born and raised in São Paulo. I am clearly a country boy, born in São Paulo but raised in the farmland. Despite our differences, Tony and I become friends almost instantly. My father invites Tony, his mother, and his sister to our house for carnival weekend. I sleep over at his house some weekends and we escape to the arcades. He knows his way through the city; he has street smarts that I am severely lacking, but I am eager to learn.

I suppose it is no coincidence that this is the year I begin noticing girls. I am staying with Tony at his house on a holiday and he takes me to some of the São Paulo parties. It is immediately apparent that he knows how to talk to girls and I do not. At one party, I see a girl across the room and I elbow Tony. "I like that girl," I say.

Tony looks at her. "Yeah, I like her, too."

"Come on, man. You live here. You are around these girls all the time. This is my first São Paulo girl."

"All right, all right. Go for it."

"Okay," I say, "but I need help. What do I do?"

He rolls his eyes. "Just go up and talk to her!" After another hour, I still have not mustered up the courage. We leave the party and I never do get a chance to talk to her. That night, Tony and I are sitting in his room and he gives me tips for approaching the girl. First, he writes a love letter for me to give to the girl. He hands it to me. "Just walk up to her and give her this," he says.

"That's never going to work!"

"Trust me."

The next day I give her the letter as Tony has instructed. Hours later, she calls Tony's house to speak to me. He holds out the phone to me. My reaction: "Oh shit. What do I say?"

"Ask her what she wants." Unfortunately, he is not aware that I need more coaching than that.

I take the phone and in a less-than-suave voice say, "What do you want?"

Tony slaps his hand against his forehead. "Not like that!" he whispers. "Ask her nicely!"

"What do you mean?" I whisper back.

"Ask her if she wants to go out. But first ask her how she is doing!"

"Oh. It would have been helpful if you had told me that before you handed me the phone!"

I hold the phone back up to my ear. "So, how are you doing?"

"Uhhh . . ." I can tell that this is not going to go far. The engine has stalled before I have left the pits.

The next morning, I get back to the track, back where I know what I am doing. It is race day and my parents and Kati have driven in from Ribeirão Preto. Kati has brought along five of her friends and they are wearing shirts with my name on them. Suddenly I have a lot more friends. The other drivers ask, "Who are the girls?"

"It's just my sister and her friends." The guys all want me to introduce them. When the race starts, I hear the girls chanting, "He-li-o! He-li-o!" I want to kill them. Kati is the loudest of all and though I pretend to be annoyed, I am happy to hear her voice. Once I am at the starting line, the noise from the go-karts drowns out any other sound. At last I am comfortable. The starter drops the green flag and I go off.

At the first turn, I see my father with his two index fingers at his temples. *Stay focused. Use your head. You don't have to win it in the first lap.* I am usually impatient and I want to be out front for the whole race, but this time I stay in the middle of the pack and wait until the final laps to make my move. When there is a clear opening, I go for it, moving to the outside, accelerating at full throttle, and passing the three cars in front of me. I am out in front and have to maintain the lead for two laps. I see Dad pointing to his temples, I see Kati and her friends whooping and jumping up and down, and I see Mom, praying, of course. I begin the last lap. There are two guys on my tail, but I know that as long as I keep my focus, there is no way I am losing. When I cross the line in first, I realize that this is the first time I have truly followed Dad's advice. Stay focused. Use your head. You don't have to win it in the first lap. I adhere to the advice for the rest of the season and end up winning a few major races and I come in second in the Brazilian Karting Championships. I have tasted a piece of the pie and now I want all of it. I put myself on a mission to be at the top of the podium next year.

I begin to head to São Paulo on Wednesday mornings now, only going to school on Mondays and Tuesdays. Most often my father drives me, but now he is comfortable to leave me in the city to stay with the mechanics or at Tony's house and he goes back to Ribeirão Preto to work until the weekend. Sometimes a mechanic drives me; otherwise I take the bus.

Every so often, Mom drops me off. I know it makes her nervous that I am missing so much school and she tells me, "Helio, if you don't keep your grades up, I'll take you right out of racing." I know that she is not fooling around, so I do everything possible to maintain a passing average—I study on the way to São Paulo and then I stay at school late on Mondays and Tuesdays, taking all the tests for the week. As long as I am passing, Mom doesn't say much. It seems that she is more comfortable with the racing, perhaps because now there is evidence of my talent. There are racks of trophies, awards, and articles from the São Paulo papers. If you want to know the truth, I think she is starting to like it almost as much as my dad does. I know Kati does. Neither of them misses a single race. Mom generally stays quiet, but Kati is always cheering the loudest on the sidelines. She has learned the rules and the strategies, and often I see her explaining things to my mother and grandmothers. Kati sits with me to watch Formula One on TV and asks me to explain the races to her. "Why doesn't he just pass him now?" she says.

I find myself repeating my father's words: "You don't win a race in the first lap, Kati. You have to wait for the right opening."

One afternoon in late May, we are watching the Indianapolis 500, an American CART series race. "What is the difference between Formula One and CART?" Kati wants to know.

"The cars are a little different. They are lighter in Formula One. And Formula One doesn't have oval courses like this." I point to the TV. Coverage of the 1989 Indianapolis 500 rolls and the camera pans across the huge oval track. I am not used to seeing the oval—we don't race ovals in Brazil and most of the races I watch on TV are Formula One. In South America and Europe, IndyCar is not nearly as popular as Formula One. Formula One is our Mecca—our second religion. At any given time of the day, there is an F1 race on TV. But we are watching the Indy 500 because Emerson Fittipaldi is racing, and Emerson Fittipaldi is a Brazilian legend.

Dad comes in the family room and sits on the couch with us.

He explains to us how dominant Emerson was when he raced in Formula One in the 1970s. "There was nobody like him," he tells us. I know this story already. I know all about Emerson. I have seen his name and face on posters and magazine covers since before I can remember. Dad also better explains the difference between IndyCar and Formula One (or Grand Prix racing). "The cars look the same, but these IndyCars have turbocharged engines, so they are more powerful than the Grand Prix cars. They go faster in a straight line, but the Grand Prix cars are lighter and quicker so they can navigate all the turns in the road courses."

"Are the ovals easier?" I ask.

"Some say yes; some say no. I wouldn't know. I've never driven an oval."

The race begins and we all focus on Emerson, who is driving a red and white Team Penske car with the Marlboro logo across the side. I notice that the camera often pans to a white-haired man in a white jacket. "Who is that?" I ask Dad.

"Roger Penske. He was a big driver in the sixties; now he owns Team Penske. That's who Emerson is racing for. It's the best team in IndyCar."

Throughout the three-hour race, Mom walks in and out of the family room, pretending that she is not interested. During the final laps, she finally sits down with us. Emerson is in a dead heat with an American driver, Al Unser, Jr. Both of them are flying around the track at 220 miles per hour. The announcer is talking just as fast. "They're side by side! Emerson comes on the inside of Little Al! It's a drag race on the back side! Can Fittipaldi get past?" We are all standing up and shouting at the TV—Dad, Kati, even Mom. Just then, Emerson and Unser touch wheels and Unser slams into the wall.

"Little Al into the wall!" the announcer yells. "Emerson continues on, screaming toward the white flag!" We are not sure if it is a legal move or not and we wait to hear the announcer call out the winner. A moment later he shouts, "Brazilian Emerson Fittipaldi is the first non-American to

win the Indianapolis Five Hundred in over twenty years!"
We all stand up and cheer as we watch Emerson take the
victory lap.

We sit back on the couch to watch the postrace coverage.
Mom stays for a minute or two before going off to make dinner. Kati and Dad stay for ten minutes more, watching the
winner's circle proceedings. The track official puts a wreath
around Emerson and hands him a carton of milk. "Why are
they giving him milk?" I ask.

"It's some kind of tradition. This is a big American race.
There are a lot of old traditions that go along with it."

Soon Kati and Dad leave, but I sit there for at least another
hour, waiting for the one-on-one interview with Emerson.
When he appears onscreen, he looks older than I expect.
His skin is deeply tanned and there are grooves in his face
that never appeared on his old Formula One posters. His
hair is still stylishly long but it now has streaks of gray. And
he is also more solemn than I expect. "I am very emotional,"
he says. "This was the best win of my career. I've dreamed
about it since I was a little boy" This shocks me—I am still
unconvinced that this Indy race is bigger than any European
Grand Prix.

Emerson and the reporter go on to discuss his past Formula One days and the "second coming" he is experiencing
now in the American CART series. "I am forty-four, but I feel
like I am twenty-two," he says. "I have started to pay more
attention to my diet. I eat mostly complex carbohydrates—
barley, wheat, whole grains. I don't eat red meat—I will have
a bit of poultry or fish."

"It sounds like a marathon runner's diet."

"Yes, well, driving is a lot more physical than most people
realize."

I am making mental notes of Emerson's diet and habits.

Drink lots of water, eat mostly carbohydrates, load up four days before a race on even more carbohydrates.

I walk into the kitchen and announce, "Mom, I'm not eating red meat anymore."

"What do you mean? Why not?"

"It is for my training. I need complex carbohydrates."

"Complex carbohydrates?"

"Yes."

"And what will you eat for protein?"

"A little bit of fish and chicken."

"What is wrong with this kid?" she mumbles to herself as she places the Sunday meal on the table—*churrasco com feijão y arroz* (grilled steak with beans and rice). As we eat dinner, Mom studies me as I pile my plate with rice and beans. I know she is debating whether to fight me on the red meat issue, but she doesn't say anything. The following night, she cooks chicken for me. Every night after that, she always has a chicken or fish dish set aside for me.

By the end of the 1989 season, my mother becomes a full racing convert. I have won five of the six major races and when it comes down to the Brazilian Championship, Mom seems to be the most intense of us all.

My name has been appearing in the national newspapers for the past week: "Helio Castro Neves—Favorite to Win the Brazilian Championship," one headline reads. We drive to the south of Brazil, to Taruma, for the championship race. There are three qualifying heats to determine where we will start the race. I win the first heat; then a local driver from Taruma wins the second and third. The Taruma driver is incredibly quick and I know he is going to be my biggest challenge.

I start in third place and the Taruma driver starts in first. The whole race I am riding his tail. He is impossibly fast, so fast that it makes me suspicious of his car. I wonder if it meets the regulations. I have been racing for three years and I have never seen a guy as fierce. I am doing everything I can to pass him. I realize that he is too strong on the straight-aways so I am going to have to make my move on a corner. I enter the corner at a furious speed and end up clipping the curb and putting myself in danger. It is my last-ditch effort and it doesn't work. In the end, the Taruma driver wins the championship and I come in second.

As soon as we finish, our cars go through the standard inspection. "Something is up with his car," I tell my father. "I can tell." The track officials have a measurment tool that they pass through the carburetor hole to make sure that it meets regulations. The larger the hole, the more air that gets into the carburetor, which makes the car go faster. It has to be small enough to meet the regulations. If the tool passes through, the hole is too big and the driver is disqualified. I suspect that the Taruma driver's carburetor hole is larger than the limit. I watch as the judges inspect his car. I am sure that the tool is going to pass through, and I am surprised when it does not. Then I see the judge kneeling down and looking further at the hole. "I can see light on the sides of it," he tells the other judge. Two more judges kneel down to inspect and they realize that the hole is in fact an oval.

It is about three o'clock and they cannot declare the winner because they have to investigate the situation further. I tell my parents to drive back to Ribeirão Preto and I will stay and await the result. At 9 p.m., the judges finally declare me the winner—I am Brazilian national champion. I stand on the podium under the moonlight as they hand me my trophy.

When I get back to Ribeirão Preto the following morning, the local press is waiting to speak with me. My publicist, Americo, puts my picture in the national paper with a full-page article. Everybody in my hometown tells me congratulations when they see me. The feeling of being a champion has entered my bloodstream. I start to believe what my father believes, that I really can make it to the top level. This is no longer just a sport—it is now a quest.

In the off-season, from October 1989 through March 1989, I begin to train for the first time. At fourteen, my mother thinks I am still too young for weight lifting. "Your muscles will atrophy," she says. I have no idea what she means, but it scares me enough to keep me away from the weights a little longer. Instead I take up tennis and sign up for lessons at the local club. "Can you throw the ball so I can run a lot?" I ask my instructor. He looks at me like I am nuts. I am not very interested in learning the technique; I just want to sweat and build up my endurance. After my lesson, I run the four miles back home.

Once I have been practicing a few weeks, my instructor enters me in a tournament at the club. I play against a kid five years younger than me and he kicks my ass. My competitive spirit kicks in, but it does me no good since I don't have the skill. Clearly, I have not missed my calling. I head to an abandoned dirt track every day after school and run sprints and drills. My mother thinks I am crazy. Dad is supportive and encouraging, but he is never the one telling me that I have to run or work out. It is born of my own determination. I am in control and it is a great feeling. When the season starts up in March, I think that I am ready.

ſ

We now have a flatbed truck, which carries my go-kart, my spare go-kart, four engines, and two sets of spare tires. One Saturday, my dad and I head out to a practice track at Campinas with two of my mechanics. When we get to the track, it is closed.

"For what?" my dad asks the track manager.

"In the next city there is a fifty-mile go-kart race," he tells us.

"Where is the next city?"

"Limeira City. It's about seventy-five kilometers from here."

My father asks me, "Do you want to go?"

"For sure," I say. We all hop back in the truck and drive on toward Limeira City. When we get there, the race officials tell us, "I'm sorry, but it is two drivers per team. It is a hundred-mile race."

Dad puts his hand on my shoulder. "Do you want to do it alone?"

"Yes."

"Okay, we would still like to enter," Dad tells the official.

"It is a hundred-mile race. He won't be able to do it alone."

"Is it against the rules? Or you just don't think he can do it?"

The race officials all turn to each other and huddle to discuss the situation. I hear them asking each other in muffled voices, "Is it against the rules?"

"I suppose not, but I don't think he will be able to do it."

"Should we allow it?"

They come out of their huddle and the head official says to us, "Okay, we can let you enter alone, but you will still have to pay the fee for two drivers."

"That is fine," my father tells him.

"Do I get two trophies if I win?" I want to know.

"Sure, son," the man tells me. "If you win, you will get two trophies." I can sense that he doesn't think I will finish, let alone win. I am determined to prove him wrong.

Before the race starts, I make a bet with my dad, since it is becoming a tradition to make a prerace bet. "If I win," I say, "I get to drive all the way back to Ribeirão Preto."

We are ninety miles from home and I do not yet have my license. He smiles and puts his hand out for me to shake. "Okay, deal," he says. I can sense that he is confident I will not only finish, but win handily.

The race begins and I jump out in front. My father is giving me signs on the side—his fingers are at his temples right away. When the time comes to switch with our racing partners, I jump out of my first go-kart and into my spare. I fly back out of the pits and my mechanics prep and gas up my first go-kart. When it is time to switch again, I hop out of the spare and jump into the first kart again.

Halfway through the race, my arms begin to grow tired and the buzzing of the go-kart becomes maddening. The go-karts of the 1980s are still primitive; there are no silencers on the engines and they don't ride as smoothly as later machines do. If you spin out, you need someone to push you back to restart. Two hours behind the wheel is punishing, but I am in the lead and not about to give up. There is perhaps another hour to go and I am four laps ahead of everyone else. With nearly half an hour to go, I have stretched it to five laps. When I come across the finish line, I am six laps ahead of the next driver. Everybody looks amazed except for Dad and my mechanics. They pat me on the head and tell me "good job." The head official comes over to shake my hand. I feel that I have just proven my talent, not to anybody else, but to myself.

I don't drive home after all. Instead I fall asleep in the passenger seat, with the buzzing noise still in my head and with two trophies tucked at my feet.

∫

In 1990, instead of defending the National Championship in Brazil, I decide to go to the World Cup in Italy. I want to step outside Brazil and get a feel for European racing, and the World Cup is the most prominent international karting race. My parents, Kati, and I fly to Lonato, in the province of Brescia, fifteen days before the race. My dad has rented out a go-kart facility and a team of mechanics. We spend the first few days at the facility, meeting the mechanics, and I am learning the differences between the Brazilian karts and the European karts. The European karts are more sophisticated and more powerful than the Brazilian karts I am accustomed to driving. We do not speak Italian or English, but we are all able to communicate through racing terms. The mechanics explain to me that these karts have a better grip than I am used to, so I have to learn to brake deeper. I spend a week getting the hang of braking a fraction of a second sooner and then accelerating at the top of the corner.

A week before the race, we go to the registration hall to get my papers. "Helio Castro Neves," my father tells the man behind the check-in table.

The man flips through his papers, then looks up and shakes his head at us. "I'm sorry, but we do not have your documentation."

My father tries my full name. "Helio Alves de Castro Neves?"

The man shakes his head again. "We don't have any papers for a Castro Neves."

"I'm sorry. What? Kati, what is he saying?"

"He said he doesn't have Helio's papers."

"That is not possible. We sent it in months ago. Through the CBA."

He shuffles the papers again. "I'm sorry, sir, but it is not here."

The only way to find out what happened is to call the head of the CBA (Confederacao Brasilieira de Automobilismo— the Brazilian Autosport Confederation). My father finds a pay phone and Kati and I watch him as he speaks to the president. I can tell it is not going well by the way he is flailing his arms and the increasing volume of his voice. Mom stands by, as usual, gripping her rosary.

Dad cups the phone and informs us that the president told him there had been a mistake at the office and they never sent my papers.

My father uncups his hand from the phone receiver again. "Why didn't you tell me?" he asks the man. "We flew all the way here. I rented out an entire go-kart facility."

The CBA president apologizes, but says there is nothing he can do. He has just learned of the situation himself. Dad is more frustrated than I have ever seen him. He hangs up the phone, takes a deep breath, and returns to the registration table. "There must be something we can do," he says pleadingly to the head official.

"The only possibility now is for you to go speak with the Ernest Buser, the president of the International Karting Commission."

"Okay, great. Where is he?"

"In Switzerland. Tomorrow is Saturday. He is not working; he will be at his home. He is German. Do any of you speak German?"

We all pause for a moment. Then Kati says, "Yes, I can speak German. Let's go." In reality she can only speak a very little bit. But she can also speak some French and a bit of English. She tells me she will figure out some way to get by.

My father springs into action. "Okay, we need a map. Where can we find a map?" A map of Europe appears from somewhere and everybody in the hall starts to crowd around and tell us how to get to Ernest Buser's. There are nine different languages flying around. People are pointing up and down, left then right. Jan Magnussen, a Danish driver, introduces himself and says he can help. I recognize his name

and recall that he is the reigning world champion. Jan shows
us the most direct route. He runs his finger along a road
from Lonato to Milan, then on an autostrada (freeway)
from Milan up over the Alps. Through hand gestures and
head nods, we eventually understand how to get from the
Alps to Ernest Buser's hometown.

My parents, Kati, and I set off for Switzerland at four in
the morning. I am not quite sure how we find our way to
Ernest Buser's home. It is some kind of miracle. He lives in
a tucked-away little cottage in a suburb of Zurich. Dad, Kati,
and I knock on his door at eight-thirty in the morning—
Mom decides she will be of more use if she stays in the car
and prays. Mr. Buser answers the door in his pajamas, with
a confused look on his face. We depend on Kati to explain
our situation. She starts to explain why we are there, or she
attempts to, anyway. In one sentence she uses four languages.
He invites us in and gestures for us to sit at his dining room
table. He and Kati start to speak, but I do not understand
most of what they say. I just bow my head and pray the rosary
as they converse in a messy mix of languages. Finally, Kati
says to my father and me, "Okay, he says there is nothing
he can do now. All one hundred fifty spots are filled. But if
somebody gets hurt or drops out, he will do everything to
make sure you can replace that seat."

There is nothing for us to do then but thank him and
join Mom in her prayers. We drive back to Italy and I start
practicing in hopes that there will be an opening. I become
friends with a Colombian driver, Juan Pablo Montoya. And
my father becomes friends with his father. Since our languages are similar enough, we are able to communicate. Juan
Pablo is a madman. During practice, there is a big mash-up
and one kart goes flipping over the others. I stop to watch
and sure enough, Juan Pablo emerges from the flipping

kart. Not an hour later, the exact scene occurs again. "Man," I tell him, "you've got to take it easy." It is the first time I have seen a guy drive like that and I am fascinated. I start to get acquainted with some of the other drivers as well—guys from Italy, France, Germany, Sweden. We are able to communicate through the common language of racing. My eyes are opening up to the world beyond Brazil.

Two days before the race, a call comes from Buser. "One of the drivers has broken his arm. He can't race. You are in, kid." I place sixteenth out of the hundred and fifty drivers, which I am pretty proud of, considering I was never supposed to race at all. A French driver, Jeremy Dufour, comes in first.

The next year, the go-kart World Cup is in France. I decide that I want to go again, but this time we make sure to get everything in order and follow up several times. The Friday before we leave for France, I go to school. It is the middle of the school year, and this is the first time I have been at school on a Friday. I still take all of my tests on Mondays and Tuesdays; then I race the rest of the week. My teachers allow me to bring all my work home, and as long as I keep my grades up, everyone is okay with it.

This Friday, I am sitting in a study hall and the monitor asks me, "Are you new?"

"No," I tell him.

"I haven't seen you here before."

"Well, I am usually racing on Fridays."

"Every Friday? Are you sure that is a good idea? You should be in school. You should be studying and preparing for your future."

"He is going to the World Cup next week," one of my friends tells the monitor. "In France."

"Oh, so you're good?"

I shrug.

My friend pipes up again. "He went to the World Cup last year, too."

"Oh, well, then. If you are good, you should keep going! Let us know how you do."

"Okay," I say, and continue to stare at the clock, waiting for the final bell to ring, when Dad will pick me up to go to the airport.

Before we get on the plane, Dad calls once more to make sure everything is all set. Only my father and I are going this time. Kati has become very serious with her ballet and is traveling around Brazil with the national company. My father encourages my mother to go with her, probably so she will not see how much money he is spending on the go-karts. Dad and I head off to France, where everything goes much more smoothly with my registration than at the last World Cup. However, this time I have a bit of trouble trying to transition to the more sophisticated European go-karts. "The cars have a lot more power," I tell my father. "I know I have to brake later, but I can't get it right."

I am getting more and more frustrated with each passing day and Dad keeps repeating to me, "Keep your head about you."

But I do not listen and I let the frustration get the best of me. I do not fare too well in the race and instead of berating me, Dad calmly tells me, "You got inside of your own head. You doubted yourself and once you doubt yourself, there is no way you are going to do well."

When we get back to Brazil, I remember these words and remind myself of them at each starting line. I end up winning nearly every race for the remainder of the season and cannot help but think it has something to do with my father's words.

ſ

At the end of the 1991 season, I am sixteen and ready for the next step. I have been promoted to the A Series and have had a very successful year. I overhear my parents one night and discover that my father has spent over four hundred thousand dollars on my go-karting. This makes my mother nervous, but I know and my father knows that this is just the beginning.

Nobody dreams of only being the top of the Brazilian A Series. I move on to Formula Chevrolet, a new series they are developing for drivers who have finished go-karts. In order to prepare for the new challenge and the heavier cars, I decide that now is the time for me to start lifting weights. I ask a trainer in São Paulo, Silviano Domingues, to help me. He has trained drivers as young as thirteen. His background is in track and field, but he tells me that the training for racing is just the same. Silviano develops a program for me and writes it out on a sheet of paper. I am to take it to my local gym and work out on my own and then report back to him each week. My family belongs to the local recreation center, where there is a pool, basketball and tennis courts, and soccer fields. There is also a small gym in the basement of the complex. It is dark and musty. The weights are old and unused—weight lifting is not a very popular activity. But I retreat to this basement gym each day and go through my regime—squats, bench presses, curls, sit-ups, push-ups, chin-ups. Afterward I head to the abandoned track and run my sprints and drills.

After a few weeks, I start to notice that I have a better handle on the car and my endurance is improving. I am in São Paulo working with Silviano. "You must focus on your shoulders and neck," he says. "That is the most important for a driver. And your endurance—we have to start to work on your endurance." He hands me a heart rate monitor and tells me to wear it during my next race. "You want to be around one-twenty for most of the time and then one-fifty to one-sixty during the extreme moments." During the first lap of my next race, my heart rate is 222. I am so distracted during the next few laps, eventually I rip off the monitor and vow never to wear it again.

Dad and I soon discover that in Formula Chevrolet, money really starts to talk. Arisco, one of the top teams, is interested in me. My friend Tony Kanaan has just signed on with them and I am excited that we are going to be teammates. However, in order to drive with Arisco, the team asks for two hundred thousand dollars. "No way," my dad says. "For that amount I can buy my own team."

I plead with him: "Dad, are you sure you know what you are talking about? Let's go with this team. It is the best team in the league." But he has made up his mind. I can tell that there is no arguing with him. He hires the same mechanics who had been with him when he owned the stock car team and some of the mechanics from my go-kart team. We buy a Formula Chevrolet car, and now my father is spending even bigger money. Formula Chevrolet cars are much more sophisticated than go-karts—the engines are significantly larger, the body has wings to control the balance of the car, and the wheels are outside the main body (aka "open-wheel cars"). In addition, Formula Chevrolet tracks are larger and more complex. It is possible, and actually quite common, for a driver to be very good at go-karts and not so good at Formula Chevrolet. I am having trouble figuring out the transition. I worry that I will not be able to make the next step.

In my first Formula Chevrolet race, I am all over the track. I cannot keep the car straight. I wonder if this is the end for me. Luckily, Alfredo Guaraná Menezes, or "Tío Guaraná," sees the race on TV. Nobody has heard from Alfredo in five years, but all of a sudden he is on the telephone line asking to speak to me. "Hey, Helinho," he says. "You looked pretty bad out there."

"I know," I say, dejected. "It's not the same as go-karts."

"I can help. Let me speak to your dad." My dad and Alfredo were friends for years but have not spoken in a while. Dad is happy to hear from him. They both agree that Alfredo should join our team as my engineer. Now I am a sixteen-year-old boy with a full team of mechanics and an engineer behind me. I figure out the transition almost immediately after Alfredo comes on board. He knows every track and every trick. "Helinho," he will say, "I know this starter. He always, always lets the flag go on three one-thousand. As soon as he lifts his arm, you count, one-one-thousand, two-one-thousand, three-one-thousand, and then you step on it."

"But, Alfredo—"

"No buts. Three-one-thousand and you go. Don't wait to see the green flag being thrown; just step on it."

So, on three-one-thousand, without looking at the starter, I step on it. The green flag is waved and I fly into the lead.

I am pumped, but then I realize I never asked Alfredo what to do after the start. I step on the gas, but I lose the lead pretty quickly and end up finishing in the middle of the pack. But Alfredo has gained my trust. From then on, I listen to everything he says. Sometimes I challenge him on certain strategies, yet in the end I follow his instruction.

With his help, I finish second in the Brazilian championship. I come in behind the dominant Texaco team, but ahead of Arisco, the team that had asked for so much money. My father has spent over $250,000, even more than Arisco had asked him to invest. And, of course, the quest is not over. In fact, it has barely begun.

∫

After Formula Chevrolet, I take the next step to Formula Three South America. The Formula Three cars are even more sophisticated than those in Formula Chevrolet, and of course, the money gets even steeper. In 1993, one of the biggest Formula Three teams, Augusto Cesario, approaches my father and me. They ask me to come and test with them. I am excited, because this is the team that had won the national championship in 1992. "Okay," my dad says. "Let's go. Let's see what it's about." During my test, I beat the team's record. They are impressed, and they ask me to drive for them. However, they also ask for $250,000. "No way," my dad says again. "For that money I can make my own team."

"Not again, Dad!" I say. "You are crazy. They have the best cars. They have computers! They have all of the high-tech equipment that we can't afford." But by this time I know that there is no reasoning with him once he makes up his mind. I soon discover that he is not only trying to protect my career; he is also running out of money. He sells two more of his properties and hires another mechanic, João, who worked for the national champion the year before. Then we go in search of a Formula Three car. We cannot afford to buy a new one, so we are looking for a good secondhand model. In Formula Three, the rule is that the chassis (body of the car) has to be three years old. In 1993, the best available chassis is a 1990 model. Most of the other drivers have the 1990 chassis, but we cannot find one on the secondhand market. A friend of a friend comes through with an old, beat-up 1988 car. It is in horrible shape, but it our only option. With only a week before the first race, we purchase the car and have a new engine built for it. When we bring the car to the team, João stares at it for a while. He then looks at my father. "You're kidding, right?" he asks.

Dad shrugs his shoulders. "It is the best I could find. It will have to do."

We get to the first race and all the other teams have computers and fancy equipment. Meanwhile, we have our banged-up old car, which we have painted all black to hide its defects. Instead of having a sponsor's logo, we have painted a big white question mark on the side.

Open-wheel cars are assembled with the suspension on the side and the engine supporting the whole structure. For the maximum performance potential, an open-wheel car needs to be stiff and inflexible. The newer cars use unbendable carbon fiber to build the chassis, but our chassis is older and made of an aluminum honeycomb structure. There are rivets in the middle, attaching the engine to the body.

Before the first race, we are having issues with the car. It feels loose and unstable. No matter how hard I push, I cannot qualify any higher than twelfth out of twenty-five. I am frustrated because I know that if I only had a better car, I would be in the top group. "Concentrate," my father tells me. "We have to work with what we have. Do not focus on what you cannot control."

I try to follow his advice and head out for the prerace practice. After only two laps, the car literally falls apart. As I turn a corner into the second lap, the rivets come undone and the car begins to break in half. I pull into the pit lane. "What do we do now?" I ask. My mechanics work quickly to bolt the car back together; it isn't the ideal fix but it is the only option. As they are working, I pace on the side in frustration. When I look up to the sky, I notice a huge, dark cloud on the horizon. "Excuse me," I ask a local fan, "what do you think about that cloud over there? Is there going to be rain?"

"Well, nine times out of ten a cloud like that means there is going to be a downpour. I'd guess it's coming in about thirty minutes."

This is great news for me. When it rains, there is no benefit to having a stiff car. The track is slippery and parts of it become like ice. Racing strategy completely shifts to avoid spinouts and hydroplaning. You have to take the corners at a much slower speed and this changes the entire race. A flexible car is an advantage in these conditions. I run back to my team and tell them, "It's going to rain. I asked a local and he said it will probably start in thirty minutes. We should set up the car for rain." It is a gamble. If it doesn't rain, we are in trouble. But we all talk it over and figure we have nothing to lose. The mechanics work to loosen up the car and switch the gearbox and we all wish for the black cloud to come toward us.

Right before the race begins, the sky opens up and rain starts to come down in buckets. We have no radio; instead my father and the rest of my crew will give me signs by holding up long pieces of bamboo on the side of the track.

The race begins with a standing start, which means all of us are on the line, completely still and waiting for the red light to turn to green. When the light changes, I push on my clutch and my car immediately stalls. I wave my arms to let the officials know to stop the race. They halt all the drivers and my coach runs to me.

"What happened?"

"It's stalling."

"Okay, try it again."

On the second start, it stalls again and I wave my arms once more. My coach and the head track official come to the side of my car. The official tells me, "Buddy, if you do it again, I'm going to make you start from the pits."

"Tío, what do I do?" I say. "I have no clutch."

"As soon as the light turns green, put it in first gear instead of pressing on the clutch."

We line up once more and when the light turns green, I do as I am told. Right away I start passing people and go from twelfth to fifth on the first lap. Since everything on my car is outdated, I have no telemetry to measure and report the mechanical data. More important, I have no radio to communicate with my team. In go-karts, I could see my dad and my mechanics standing only two or three feet from the track, giving me signs. But now there is a twenty-yard gap between the pits and the track. The only way for my team to communicate is to hold out a long bamboo stick with a plus or minus sign on it, meaning "speed up" or "slow down." In addition to all the new changes and trying to see in the rain without a visor, I have to learn to use my peripheral vision to look for the sign at the corner of the track.

With ten laps to go in the race, I am in second place and I see the bamboo stick with a minus sign. Why are they telling me to slow down now? I ease up on the gas but for five laps the minus sign is still out there. I have dropped to fourth place. Then with three laps to go, they switch to plus and I gun it and regain second place and battle for the lead for the last two laps. A veteran Formula Three driver edges me out at the finish and I place in second.

I think I am happier than the winner—my team and my dad are also overjoyed at the result. Nobody expected me to do so well. A lot of fans are congratulating me and I know that I have made an impression in my first race. "We got lucky today," my dad says, "but it is not going to rain every time. We have to fix this car. We can't make fools of ourselves now." He sends the car to a guy he knows who builds airplanes. The man makes the car strong and adds wings to increase the aerodynamics.

The next race is in Interlage, São Paulo. All of my friends come to the race and I want to show them what I can do. I start the race in the third position and after a few laps, I pass two cars in one corner. I am leading the race, but the clutch is acting up and I can tell that something is wrong. On a corner, when I downshift, the brake pedal goes all the way to the floor. I am not sure what is happening. I spin out, though I am able to keep the car straight. Still, I lose two positions and I am pissed. I make another pass but cannot catch up to the leader. I finish in second and my team is excited again. "Good job!" my dad says.

"No! That was my race!" I say. I explain what happened with the car and we have to tweak it some more. Throughout the season, we continue to alter the car, trying to get it perfect. It is a process of trial and error, but rewarding and frustrating depending on the day. I know that it would be easier if we had more money, but as it is, my father has spent $250,000 to field the team and "the banged-up old car." I am determined to make sure my father's investment is not wasted. Every spare moment I am at the track or working out at the gym.

I have my first serious girlfriend at this time and after a while she starts to try to control what I am doing. "You are always at the track," she says. "You don't have any time for me."

I am not sure how to respond. For me, racing comes before anything else. How can I tell her this in a nice way?

"You have to make a choice," she tells me. "The track or me."

Clearly this is not the girl for me. I do not skirt around the issue. Instead I tell her, "I'm sorry, but I choose the track."

It is the first instance when I choose the track over a girl, but I know it will not be the last. My trainer tells me, "The girls will always be there, the parties will always be there, but once you lose a race, you cannot get it back." With those words in my mind, I continue to devote myself to racing rather than going to parties and clubs, or going out drinking with friends. My addiction is the track, and time after time, I allow everything to fall by the wayside so that I can just drive.

Just drive.

∫

By the eighth race of the season, I am the only Brazilian with a chance to win the championship. After an incredible win with Team Corpal, a team owner named Amir Nasr, from Nasr Racing, approaches me. Nasr Racing is a top team with a lot of sponsors, high technology, and plenty of experience. Amir tells me, "We want to sign you. We'll give you a better car and take care of everything else. You just drive." There are three races to go in the season and if I win all three, I will secure the championship.

I turn to my dad and say, "Every time I doubt you, you prove me wrong. Tell me what to do."

"It's time to go, son."

∫

I make an agreement with Nasr Racing that I will race for them as long as they can find a driver to finish out the season with Team Corpal. Instead of receiving payment, I want to make sure that someone will rent my father's team, because I want my guys to be at the championship, too.

For the first time, I drive for a team that is not my father's. And for the first time, I have to learn how to deal with a whole mess of technology in my car. I didn't have a radio before, but now I have a radio, a computer, and an antenna. The antenna cuts right in the middle of my windshield and that throws me off. It all takes a bit of getting used to at the beginning, yet I realize that I am driving half as hard and going twice as fast. It is as though I were running on the sand before and now I am running on pavement.

I win the next two races and the championship title comes down to the final race. It is between an Argentinean driver, Fernando Croceri, and myself. If Croceri comes in at least second place, he will win the championship by one point. In the final lap, I am leading. All of the drivers in second to fifth place are Argentinean, Croceri is in sixth. It looks like the championship is mine. I cross the finish line first and hear my team yelling in the radio, "You are the champion! You are the champion!" However, in the next moment, the four drivers behind me stop their cars and allow Croceri to pass. He finishes second in the race, which means he is in first place in the overall championship.

I had not seen what had happened, but when I stop my car I see my team fighting. My father takes me out of the driver's seat of my car and we march toward the garage. "What is going on?" I ask Dad. "We won! Why is everyone fighting? I am the champion!"

"You are the champion for us," my dad says.

"What do you mean 'for us'?"

He explains to me what happened and it is the first time I don't go to the podium. (It was not my idea . . . It was my dad's.)

Croceri is named Formula Three champion, and I am in second place overall. We are all upset and disappointed. My dad has already spent so much money, time, and effort. I have been so focused and working so hard. Kati is the angriest of us all. She marches up to all of the Argentineans and starts screaming. "Oh yeah," she tells them, "you will all be racing in Argentina for the rest of your lives. But my brother, he will be the best race car driver in the world. You'll see." Then, thank God, a bodyguard pulls her away. If I had not been so upset, I would have found the situation comical— my little bit of a sister standing up to a huge group of drivers, shaking her finger in their faces.

After that race, we decide I am ready to leave the South American racing circuit and take the next step, which is British Formula Three. Before the 1995 season begins, my dad and I fly to England so I can do the two-day test. I do well the first day, and the second day I finish third in a race at the track. Several teams are interested in me. I sign with the premier Formula Three team, Paul Stewart Racing, which is owned by the son of the legendary Formula One driver Jackie Stewart. I finally get a sponsor, Caixa, a bank in Brazil. This has been the same sponsor for Nasr Racing. My father works out a deal with Caixa—he will take out a five-hundred-thousand-dollar loan from them, which the bank will pay out at the end of the year as part of its sponsorship. At last I think my dad is not going to have to pay for anything.

I move to England in March 1995. My mother stays with me for three months, teaching me to cook, do my laundry, go grocery shopping, make my bed (all of which have been done for me before). Neither of us speaks English nor understands the British culture. It takes us ten minutes just to communicate to my building manager that we want to find a home goods store. I want a blender so I can make my banana shakes and my mom wants to stock up on cleaning supplies. I insist that Mom and I try to get by without using the Portuguese-English dictionary. I think it is better to learn by speaking instead of constantly referring to the dictionary, but that is proving quite challenging. When the manager finally figures out what we are asking him for, he draws us a map on the back of a paper bag and hands it to us. We do not know what to do with it. In our country, if you ask a Brazilian about a home goods store, we take you there, we walk you through the aisles, help you talk to the clerk, then take you back to where we started. A map on the back of a paper bag? What is this?

We set off, wandering the streets, and after a half hour or so, my mom says, "I think we've passed this building four times." We eventually figure out the map and find our way to the store. I walk up to the front counter and then realize I don't know the right word, which is *blender.* I start to spin my finger around, mimicking the blade, hoping the clerk will understand.

"Oh, okay. I know what you are looking for," the clerk says. He goes to the back and comes out with a tabletop fan.

"No, no," I say. And I try again. This time I spin my finger and make a whirring sound.

"Oh, okay. Gotcha." He goes to the back once more and comes out with a ceiling fan.

"No," I say, shaking my head. Then I act out a full-blown charade. I peel an imaginary banana, put it in the imaginary blender, and pour in some imaginary milk. Then I press the button and spin my finger and make the whirring sound. After a few moments, I remove the blender from its stand, pour my imaginary concoction into a glass, and dip my head back and take a long, imaginary sip. "Ahh," he says. "A blender!"

Then it is my mother's turn. She wants a broom, a mop, a bucket, dish towels, and detergents. She starts to clean her way around the store until we have all of our supplies. We head back to my apartment, laughing all the way. "Next time, you have to let me bring the dictionary," she says.

"Why? It's more fun this way."

The next morning, we look out the window and see snow for the first time. We rush out to make a snowman and have a snowball fight, just as we have seen in the movies. But we don't have any mittens and our hands quickly turn to ice. We cannot figure out the word for "mittens" or even where to buy them, so that is the end of our snow games for a while.

As the weeks pass, the cold, damp weather starts to get to my mother. I can tell that she is homesick. One day I call the apartment from the track to tell her I will be home soon. I hear her sniffling and holding back tears on the other end of the line. I say to her, "Go home, Mom. It's okay. I will be fine on my own." I am homesick, too, but at least I have the track. Before she leaves, she has succeeded in teaching me to cook chicken and rice, though the beans still elude me. I am still not eating red meat, and I am now following an even more strict diet and exercise regime—running every morning, avoiding soda and alcohol, sticking to chicken and mostly healthy carbohydrates (though I cannot give up my cookies). Because of my dietary restrictions and culinary skill, my dinner options are limited to chicken and not much else. For variety, I will put an egg on top and some ketchup. It is a mess, but it is gourmet dining to me.

One night, I am watching TV, trying to pick up a few English words and eating my chicken and rice. My phone rings and when I answer I am surprised to hear a familiar voice. "Helio!"

"Tony?" It is my old racing buddy, Tony Kanaan. "How did you find my number?" I ask him.

He is driving in Italy and a friend of a friend had given him my number in England. We talk for a while about racing, and how hard it is to be away from home. I tell him how incredibly difficult it is to grasp the English language. It feels good to finally speak to someone who understands me.

"How do I call you?" I ask him.

He gives me the number of his apartment manager and says to call her and she will put me through. Then he teaches me my first Italian phrase: *Vorrei parlare con Tony.* ("I would like to speak with Tony.")

I call Tony every week or so and we trade stories and jokes. It makes me feel a little less lonely to know that I am not alone on this strange European continent.

Meanwhile, I am slowly beginning to learn English, first through racing terms and then slowly by picking up regular-life words (oftentimes through an embarrassing or awkward situation).

Juan Pablo Montoya, whom I had met at the World Cup in '91, is racing in the series below me. When I run into him I am surprised and very happy to see a familiar face. Is this a small world or what? On the weekends we go out and try to navigate the British nightlife and decipher the British women (this proves exponentially more difficult than navigating a British home goods store). We are both lonely and happy to have a friend who understands our situation.

My father flies over for every race. He arrives on the Thursday before the race, just in time for qualifiers, and then he leaves on the following Monday. I am having a very good season and end up finishing in third overall; however, midway through the season, my dad finds out that his employees have been stealing from his company and that Corpal is about to fold. On top of that, Caixa, the bank that had promised to sponsor me, has reneged. Now my father owes the half million dollars to the bank and they put a foreclosure on all of his remaining properties. I am twenty years old; my father has gambled his entire company, spent more than $2 million on me, and I have not yet made a dime of it back. Things are really taking a turn for the worse.

I have a vague awareness of my family's financial problems, but I don't know the extent of it. I know the company started to have problems when I was away in England, but I was not told about the huge loans that had been taken out to pay my team. When I return to Brazil, I see that the cars have been taken away, but my father downplays the situation. Because we still live in the same house, I do not think it is all that bad. I do not pay much attention to it and nobody wants me to pay attention. My job is to drive the car. When my father sold that first property in Rio to hire me a publicist and put up a racing team, it was just one of many sacrifices my family has made in pursuit of my dream. Yet, after that dinner conversation in 1987, I do not hear much about it. My focus and my only responsibility becomes *Look ahead, go faster, just drive.*

CHAPTER 3

Testing

**It does not matter how many times
you get knocked down, but how many
times you get up.**

—VINCE LOMBARDI

I AM SITTING IN my parents' house in Ribeirão Preto. It is early November 1995 and I have just returned from London. I am so happy to be back in the warmth of Brazil, and I intend to stay here and thaw out from the long, cold Formula Three season. Kati has found me a ten-thousand-dollar sponsorship from Philip Morris South America through one of her contacts at the university. As a result, an executive at Philip Morris calls and asks if I want to participate in an Indy Lights test. "Indy Lights?" I say. "What is that?"

He explains that it is an American series, a stepping-stone to IndyCar. A team, Tasman Motors, is looking for two drivers—one Brazilian and another Latin American.

"Where is the series?" I ask.

"It's in Phoenix, Arizona," he tells me.

"What kind of car?"

"It's an Indy car, a bit bigger than the Formula One cars you are used to; also, it will be on an oval track."

My goal at the time is Formula One, not IndyCar. I have never driven an Indy car and I have never raced on an oval track. I am thinking that this is not the test for me. Outside of the United States, F1 is the most popular form of racing. In Brazil, no matter what time of day, you can turn on the TV and find a Formula One race. IndyCar was not nearly as popular when I was growing up. It has only recently become visible because a good number of Brazilian drivers, including Fittipaldi and Nelson Piquet, started to race in the Indy Racing League (IRL) once their F1 careers were over. But still, my sights are set on Formula One. I plan to go back to England and continue working my way up the ladder. I have just started to acclimate myself to the British ways. I know the system. I know the roads. I have somewhat figured out the language. I am not sure that I am ready to do that all over again in America.

"Nine other drivers are going," my sponsor says. "Five other Brazilians."

Well, maybe I will go then? I'm not one to turn down a competition. I don't think I want to race in Indy Lights, but I do want to beat those nine other drivers. Plus, it will be good experience to drive an Indy car and try out an oval. I have nothing to lose, I figure, so I agree to do the test.

Later that day, I go to the go-kart track with my friends to race for fun. I am excited to be back in a go-kart, because my contract with Jackie Stewart had forbidden me from driving them. We race each other around the track for hours. The seat is digging into my side and starting to hurt more and more, but I am having so much fun that I ignore it. As soon as I get out of the kart, I feel a severe shooting pain in my ribs. Every time I breathe in, the pain shoots up my side (now I understand why go-karting was forbidden in my contract). It is okay, I say to myself; in two weeks I will be fine. I don't tell anyone except Tony Kanaan, who is also going to the test.

Two weeks pass and my ribs are hurting more than before. I get on the plane with the intention to just suck it up and drive.

I land in Phoenix and as soon as I get off the plane, I am enamored with the place. The heat and the sunshine comfort me. It is the first time I have been to the States and it is not at all what I expected. On the drive from the airport to the track, I gaze out the window at the fast-food restaurants and the strip malls. I have the feeling that everything I want is just at my fingertips.

My attitude shifts. I could definitely live in America, I think. When I arrive at the track in Phoenix, I look around and absorb the heat and sunshine. I turn to Tony and say, "Hey, man, don't tell anyone about my ribs." We stand on the sideline, watching the other drivers. A few Americans are standing with us. I cannot understand one bit of English they are speaking. All the words are running together. Kevin Schwantz, a champion motorcycle driver, starts talking to me. He is from California and speaks in that surfer-boy lingo that completely mystifies me. We talk for at least ten minutes and the whole time I just nod my head and smile. After he leaves I turn to Tony and say, "I don't know what language I learned in England, but if that guy was speaking English, I didn't learn English."

I am the last driver in line to test and as I watch the other nine guys drive, I try to forget about the shooting pain. When it is my turn, I get in the car and remind myself to focus. It is my first time on an oval and right away I realize that it is not as easy as it looks. Making the fast turns is punishing on my neck and ribs. After ten laps, I post the fastest time of anyone, but I have to stop. I cannot breathe. Every time I take a turn, it feels like I have a knife in my side. Steve Horne, the owner of Tasman Motorsport, comes up to the side of the car. "What's wrong?" he says.

"I don't have enough air," I tell him. When I fully catch my breath I tell him about my ribs.

"Why did you come to the test?" he asks.

"I wanted to try. I thought it would be okay."

"Okay," he says. "It's a four-day test. Take a break and then come back on the last day and try again." Steve is a man with an amazing talent in motor sports. From the moment we meet, I sense that he is a great guy and that he believes in me.

I make friends with another Brazilian driver, Oswaldo Negri. We have so much in common and we bond immediately. We trade war stories from our racing experiences in England. He has so many great stories, I tell him he should write his own book. When he sees that I am having trouble, he says, "I'll help you. I'll take you to this massage place." Wow, what a great guy, I think. Usually when you are at a test, you don't make friends with the guys you are going against, let alone help them out. Oswaldo and I navigate our way through the downtown streets, asking directions along the way. He speaks a bit better English than I do because he had been racing Formula Three for several years. Phoenix is unlike any Brazilian city and I am in awe as we navigate the desert in search of the place.

When I meet the masseur, I am too unsure of my English and desperate for his help, so I do not indicate how badly my ribs are hurting. I figure he will know what to do. I get up on the table and pray that he can help me. He starts kneading his fists into my back and it feels like he is ripping me open. Be tough, I tell myself; this is good for your ribs. But eventually I can no longer take the pain. "Stop," I say. "No more." I make gestures to my ribs to explain how it is hurting too much.

He looks closely and gently presses into my side. "Oh," he says, "your ribs are broken!"

"What can I do?" I ask.

"Nothing. Just rest. Ribs have to heal themselves."

I rest for two more days, but it seems that the masseur may have caused even more damage. On the final day, I go to the track determined to complete the test. By this time everyone else is posting amazing times. I get in the car and after only three laps, I have to stop again. Steve Horne comes up to the car. "Get out," he says.

"No, I'm fine. I can do it."

"Get out." It is the same voice my father uses when he is angry with me. Oh boy, I think, I did something wrong here.

I have the sinking feeling that I have ruined my opportunity. I get out of the car and Steve puts his hand on my shoulder. "Don't worry about this test. Go home and rest. Call me at Christmas."

I cannot believe how understanding he is—will he really give me a second chance? I go back home and rest for the next two months. When the pain subsides, around mid-December, I call Steve. "I'm feeling much better," I tell him.

"Good to hear," he says, but there is no indication he wants me to come back for another test. After we hang up I think I am never going to hear from him again. By this time I have found out that my father does not have the money to support me in Formula Three next year. "Don't worry," he tells me. "I will find a way." But I don't want him to have to find a way any longer. I want to be able to stand on my own two feet.

A week later, Dad and I are driving on a back road in Brazil when we get a call on my father's cell phone. The cell phone is not too reliable to begin with, but being that we are in the middle of nowhere, it is full of static and we keep losing the connection. We drive a few hundred yards and try again. A few hundred more, and try again. Finally we get reception and we can hear the voice on the other end of the line say, "I am the president of Philip Morris South America. I would like to meet with Helio at your earliest convenience." My father turns the car around and heads straight for the company headquarters in São Paulo. We try not to get our hopes up, but we think this may be my lucky break.

Two hours later, my father and I sit down with the Philip Morris executives. "We have a situation," the president says. "You didn't pass the Indy Lights test, because you didn't complete the test. The two seats are already filled."

My heart sinks. "Tony Kanaan has secured the Brazilian seat," he tells us. "However, Steve Horne wants to make a third car for you. We will sponsor you halfway and you will have to come up with the other half, which is five hundred thousand dollars."

I look to my father. Is he going to be willing and able to do it? He stands up, offers his hand, and tells the president, "You have a deal." We all shake hands and Dad and I leave to drive back to Ribeirão Preto. Dad is silent as we make our way down the same route we have taken hundreds of times before. I watch the sun beat down on the sugarcane stalks flying by, just as I did when I was a boy.

ſ

I stare out the window of a Red Roof Inn in Dublin, Ohio. A four-lane highway; a gray sky; sleet falling on naked trees. Woohoo! I've made it! It is February 1996 and the Indy Lights season is about to begin. We have found a sponsor, Hudson Oil, to come up with the other half of my ride money and I am happy that my father will not have to be paying for it himself. I am also excited about the next chapter in my career. My mother and Kati have come to help me get situated and find a place to live. We have been in the Red Roof for fifteen days. Every morning, I wake up at seven and go for therapy for my ribs. Then we head off in search of an apartment, which is proving somewhat difficult since we barely understand this American English and we understand even less about Ohio windchill factors. I have never been so cold in my life. Every time we walk out of the car to look at another place, the wind whips around our ears. We run, laughing, to the safe harbor of the Wendy's restaurant to warm ourselves over hot chocolate—we think it is the greatest thing we have ever tasted. We eventually find a little one-bedroom apartment in Dublin. As soon as Kati and my mom help me set it up, they flee back to the warmth of Brazil.

I am on my own now, determined to figure out this foreign territory. I call my parents often. Mom wants to know if I am eating enough and if I am going to church. "Yes, I am eating; yes, I am going to church."

Dad wants to know how the racing is going. "Okay. I am learning how to drive on ovals—it's not as easy as I thought."

They send me $1,500 to buy a car, which I am grateful for since I know money is tight now. I go to the dealership and all I can afford is a 1978 Toyota Cressida. The dealer keeps telling me something about the license plates, but I don't really know what he is talking about—he just keeps pointing and asking me if I understand. I nod and say, "Okay, yes. Okay." No matter what anybody says to me, I just keep saying, "Okay, yes. Okay." I later find out that he is telling me to change the plates and register the car in my name, which I never do.

Tony and I are Brazilian comrades in Dublin, Ohio. I am thankful that we are there together—it makes it much more entertaining. But I have to admit that Tony is getting the hang of America much quicker than I am. He understands the oval tracks while I am still having a bit of trouble navigating the corners. He has a few more sponsors than I do and they have given him free plane tickets to travel around the

States. When he is gone, I mostly stay in my little apartment and I begin to wonder if this is where I belong. Should I go back to the Formula One quest?

In one of my early races, I win a small bit of prize money. When I call Dad, he tells me, "You see? You will get the hang of the oval in no time. Eventually it will become second nature." But it doesn't come so easily and I am still running in the back in most races. Meanwhile, the prize money from that early race is burning a hole in my pocket. It isn't much, but I have enough to buy a bicycle. I begin to ride my bike from my apartment to the track by taking the only route I know, Highway 275. One day, one of my mechanics sees me biking on the highway. When I get to the track he calls out to me, "Hey, man, what are you, crazy? You can't ride your bike on the Two Seventy-five!"

"Why not?"

"Because you can't ride bikes on highways!" Really? In Brazil it is normal. We even walk on the highways. Man, I am never going to understand this place.

I am frozen, my ribs are still killing me, I cannot speak the language properly, and now I am not even riding my bike the right way? The only aspect of my life that has ever remained stable is driving, but that too is eluding me in America. I cannot get the hang of the American circuits. In South America and Europe there are no ovals, only street courses. For me the learning curve is incredibly steep. Ovals require an unbelievable amount of concentration. You have to learn how to read the car, listen to what it says. It is extremely important to be comfortable in the car, but every time I strap in, my ribs ache. When I try to learn the corners, I keep crashing into the wall and every time I do, it aggravates my ribs even more. I cannot focus and after all these years I think that this may be the end of the road. I begin to get inside my own head. My team must think I don't belong here, I say to myself. They must be saying, who is this guy? He can go fast, but he has no control at all.

My confidence behind the wheel has evaporated.

I phone my parents. My mother picks up and right away I tell her, "I think I'm done. I want to come home. I'll work for Dad's company."

"Are you serious?"

"Yes," I tell her. "I gave it my best shot, but I think I've come to the end." If anyone will support me quitting, I'm sure it will be my mother. She has asked me many times to give it up, go to college, pursue something safe and secure. She will be happy I am finally following her advice.

"No," she says. "Absolutely not. You are going to stay there and you are going to stick it out. You've come this far."

"But Mom . . ."

"Hold on a moment," she tells me. I know where she is going. She is getting her Bible. When she gets back to the phone, I hear the pages flipping. She reads to me: *"Blessed is the man who perseveres under trial, because when he has stood the test, he will receive the crown of life that God has promised to those who love him. The book of James. Chapter one. Verse twelve."*

I open up my Bible to the same verse and leave it there on my bedside table.

"Thanks, Mom," I tell her. Still, I have my doubts.

The next afternoon, Steve Horne pulls me aside after practice. From that very first test in Phoenix, Steve has always had faith in me and treated me like a son. I am afraid I am letting him down. "You have the talent," he says. "That is clear."

"Thank you, but—"

"But something is wrong with your head. I'm going to help you change that. There is a clinic in Daytona Beach, Florida.

It's called HPI—Human Performance International. It will change your mentality. I promise."

Steve pays for my flight and the clinic. The first day I am there, I meet the founder, Jacques Dallaire. He looks like a physics professor and from the moment he introduces himself, I can tell he is both kind and extremely intelligent. "Don't you worry; we are going to help you. I've worked with plenty of drivers before." He gives me an "Optimist Questionnaire" with three hundred questions. Oh man, I think, where am I? Who is this guy? I don't want to take any questionnaire!

I can't understand most of the questions and I keep asking the people around me, "What does this one say?" The lady at the front desk reads to me, "If your plane was going down, would you use the parachute?"

"Yes," I answer, "of course." Wouldn't everybody? It takes me a while to finish the entire questionnaire and then I have to wait for the results. I sit, impatiently tapping my fingers, until Jacques finally comes out with his diagnosis.

"Your answers indicate that you are very negative," he says.

Very negative? Not just negative. *Very* negative. "What about the parachute question?" I ask. "How did I do on that one?"

"What do you mean, how did you do?"

"Didn't I answer it right? Wouldn't an optimist use the parachute?"

"No. An optimist is confident that he will survive the crash." It is something I never considered before and it makes me stop and think.

"Before we begin the training," Jacques tells me, "I want you to write yourself a letter about what you want to achieve here. I want you to bring it to me tomorrow."

"You want it in English?"

"Preferably, yes."

"Oh boy." I know this is not going to be easy, and especially if I have to write in English. That night, I sit at my hotel room desk in the Daytona Beach Holiday Inn and write out a conversation with God. Here it is, just as I wrote it.

> *June 10, 1996*
>
> *God,*
>
> *I am very sad and would like that situation to change. I am happy about the test and Human PI. Dan and Jack, they are very nice and look like they will show me how can I work again with the same power I had in 92, 93, and 94! I just need to know why such bad luck happened with me and why I am worried about everybody. I need to learn to be "cold like ice" and keep cool in difficult situations! Sometimes it looks like my power and that nice feeling is going away and I lose control.*
>
> *I want to be a champion. I know I have talent, feeling, and preparation to be a good driver. So I need to win for me to come back to a new world.*
>
> *Last year, for example, I won one race but I finished very well, so I know I can finish well, but I don't know how! Please show me a good way or a signal for me to follow and not always make mistakes anymore. I remember 92 when I had a problem with adaptation in the category and at the end of the championship, I finished second. 93 when I started in twelfth and finished in second on the wet. When I won my first race when the nose box broke. When I moved to a better car and I could be sick, bad, or it didn't matter the situation, when I sat in the car I was always the quickest and looked like I was unbeatable, a superman. And I would like that situation to come back!*

I worry too much about my teammates and I want to forget them and drive myself. I want to come back to F1. That's my feeling. But if I'll be there in Indy or F1, I want to give my best to win!

Thank you for my family supporting me and I just want to give the happy things for them and sometimes I am afraid to lose a sponsor so I work very hard for this not to happen. And thank you again that I am still here and I'm sorry if I said bad things sometimes, mainly in difficult situations.

Amen!!

Helio Castroneves

I hand the notepad to Jacques the following day and I watch his face as he reads the pages. I can tell that he is pleased. "This is great," he says when he gets to the end. "And don't worry. I'm going to help you. What you wrote here indicates that you are ready for the change and that is the first big step."

We begin the program directly after breakfast. Right away it is apparent that physically I am in great shape, though my rib is hurting a bit. Mentally I am a mess. I am distracted and discouraged, and of course, this is affecting my performance. Racing is 50 percent physical and 50 percent mental. I know I am not going to start winning again until I flush the negative thoughts out of my head.

Jacques give me a rubber band to put around my wrist. "Every time you have a negative thought, I want you to pull this rubber band. And you have to pull it hard. It has to hurt." He shows me how to snap it tight and it hurts like hell. I think this guy is crazy. But I keep the rubber band on for a long time, and am surprised to find that it really does work.

When I fly back to Ohio in late July, I feel focused and

confident, just like in my early racing days. I am still wearing the rubber band, but I snap it a lot less. I have managed to replace the negative thoughts with the positive. There are only three races left in the season and I am eager to get back to the track to prove myself.

The next race is in Quebec on August 4, at a new racetrack, Trois-Rivières. We head there a week before the race to practice on the new circuit. In every practice session, Tony and I trade the lead back and forth. I am not even thinking about my ribs anymore. I am just thinking about winning. During the qualifying round, I block out any doubts, any thoughts of negativity, and remind myself that all that matters is the next four laps. There is no room for error. Every fraction of a second counts. There will be no time to make up for mistakes later on.

As soon as I begin the first lap, I know that I am back. A switch has gone off in my head. I post the fastest qualifying time and capture the pole position. I know it before anybody tells me. It is my first-ever pole position and it marks a turning point in my career. After so many doubts, problems, and questions, I remember why I love this sport. And most important, I remember that I am good at it. I have my focus and self-assurance once more. I know that today, nobody can beat me.

When I am at the starting line, waiting for the green flag to drop, I talk to myself: This is what is going to happen. You are going to start in front, you are going to stay in front, and you are going to win this race. The words vibrate in my helmet. I look ahead as the green flag lifts. I grip the steering wheel. You are going to win the race. When the flag is waved, I fly out in the lead.

I hold the lead for the first lap and see Tony in my rearview, but I am cool and calm. When I cross the line, I keep my helmet on because I am crying and cannot bring myself to stop. I talk to God, thanking him for giving me this feeling back.

Steve Horne runs toward my car and is more excited than anyone. "You see?" he tells me. "I knew you had it in you!" I know that most team owners would have given up on me long ago, but not Steve. I am extraordinarily grateful that he never stopped believing in me. I find out that not only did I win the race, but I also led the most laps and recorded the fastest lap time. I feel like I have been revived from the dead. Best of all, I am having fun again. It is so easy to forget that that is the reason I got into the sport in the first place. For the fun of it! Of course I always wanted to win, but when I stopped enjoying myself, what was the point? And it is no coincidence that as soon as I stopped enjoying myself, I stopped doing well.

I call my parents, as I always do after my races. And for the first time this season I am finally able to call them with great news instead of disappointment. Then I call Jacques to thank him once again for all of his help. "You were right," I tell him. "It is unbelievable what the mind is capable of. Once my mind shifted, my ability shifted. I really can't thank you enough."

"Helio, all I did was give you the tools," Jacques says. "The rest was up to you. You should be thanking yourself."

After Trois-Rivières, I have my groove back. However, there are only two more races left in the season; I worry that my record for the entire season will not be good enough to get me a seat for next year.

The final race is in Monterey, California. Tony wins and I place in second. This means that for the entire season, Tony came in second place and I came in seventh. When Steve comes to congratulate me he says, "Listen, since Tony placed in second, he gets the full sponsorship next year. But I want you to continue to race with us as well. You have shown us your true potential. You have proven that you can work your way back from the bottom. I will make the same deal for you as we had this year. You will be covered halfway and then you come up with the other half."

"Thanks for always supporting me," I say. "I do want to race for Tasman again next season, too. I will find a way to make it work."

I call my 1996 sponsor, Hudson Oil, and luckily they agree to sponsor me again in 1997. Everything is looking up. I have my ride secured for next year, my sponsorship is covered, and I can now spend the next four months basking in the warmth of Brazil. I pack up my apartment in Dublin and board a plane for São Paulo.

My father picks me up at the airport and we take the old, familiar drive from São Paulo to Ribeirão Preto. "What's with the rubber band?" Dad asks me as we are leaving the city.

"I snap it whenever I have a negative thought. I hardly ever snap it anymore."

"How long are you going to keep it on?"

"As long as I need it, I guess. It's helped me a lot."

"What have I always told you?" Dad says. He puts his fingers up to his temples just as he has done since I was in go-karts. "Keep your head about you. Trust yourself. You are only as good as you believe."

I have a newfound understanding of those old familiar words.

Keep your head about you. Trust your own ability. Once you doubt yourself in racing, you are finished.

Sometimes it takes a period of uncertainty for you to start

believing in yourself again. And sometimes it takes a bit of going home. I stare out the windows, comforted to be on familiar terrain.

Instead of settling in, I go for a run on my old racetrack— happy to be enveloped by the Brazilian heat and humidity. With each step, I chant to myself.

Keep your head about you. Trust yourself. You are only as good as you believe.

CHAPTER 4

Slow Down

**The harder you work,
the harder it is to surrender.**
—VINCE LOMBARDI

I T IS JANUARY 1997 and the off-season is coming to a close. I am eager to get back in the car, though I am not so eager to face February in Ohio. I know that a lot of Brazilian drivers are living in Miami, even though their teams are based up north. I ask my team, Tasman Motors, and my sponsor, Hudson Oil, if I can do the same. Both agree that it is okay. The president of Hudson even tells me to stay in his vacation home in Miami for a week while I look for a place. In February 1997, I pack up my blender and head to Miami, ready to start afresh.

The president's house is a beautiful, new Mediterranean mansion. I am twenty-two years old and living the life in a land of sun and palm trees. I cannot believe my good fortune. I am both content and confident. I am sure that this is going to be my breakout year. A week later, I am sitting in the family room watching a movie when the Hudson president calls.

"Hi," I say, ready to thank him for allowing me to stay in his house.

"Helio, I am sorry but Hudson can longer sponsor you for next year."

"What do you mean?" I say. "We had a deal. What do I do now?" But I know that I am asking these questions in vain. The season has not started; we have not yet signed a contract. I am out of luck.

In one week, it seems everything has fallen apart. My sponsor has fallen through. I have no money for food or rent, and I have to turn to my father for support once again. My father is still in financial trouble, though I am not sure as to the extent of it. I wonder if he even has the money to spare. When I call and ask for support, my parents respond as they always have: "Okay. Don't worry. Just drive. We will take care of the money."

However, my father is nearly bankrupt and he owes half a million dollars to Caixa, the Brazilian bank he took out the loan from in 1995 when I was in Formula Three. Caixa had promised that as my sponsor, they would pay out the loan, but they haven't. Instead my father has ended up in massive debt. He sells his last property, the apartment where Kati is living in São Paulo, but it covers barely a tenth of the money he owes. Kati moves in with a friend so she can finish her degree. She drives back and forth between São Paulo and Ribeirão Preto every week, trying to help my father save his company. Corpal is on the brink of closing down and the bank puts a lien on our house in Ribeirão Preto.

All the while, Kati continues to search for sponsor money for me. She calls up virtually every company in Brazil and shoves my portfolio in front of anyone who will listen. Her friends tell me, "Helio, you can't believe it. Everywhere she goes, she goes with this portfolio under her arm. Everything she says is, 'My brother, my brother, my brother. He is going to be the greatest race car driver of all time. You'll see.'"

Yet I am in Miami and I have to call my parents to ask if they can send me some money for food. How did it come to this? Just a few years ago we were at the top of the world. Now we are on the brink of destitution. I feel that it is my fault—the money has been spent on my racing career and now I am not sure I will even be driving next season. I worry that I am letting everyone down.

I have to move out of the house in the next week. But where do I go from here? I have no savings and I don't even know if I will be racing this season. My team might not keep me on if I don't have a sponsor. I have become friends with the gardener of the house, Adilson Rodrigues, and I tell him of my problem. Adilson is from Rio and in the past week we have become friends. He makes me a spare key so I can stay in the house. Instead of finding an apartment, I figure that I will just wait until I know my fate. I really have no other option. I know I can't ask my father for rent money.

Adilson is my first friend in Miami. He is a great guy and he shows me the ropes of the city. He is fun and funny, but he is also the hardest worker I have ever met. He tells me he wants to build his own landscaping company and is willing to do whatever it takes to achieve that. He wakes up at four in the morning and labors until late at night.

"You are always working," I tell him.

"So are you," he says. "I am just a typical immigrant working toward the American dream. Just like you."

One afternoon I am helping Adilson install a kitchen faucet at his new house. I am upset because I am still uncertain about what I am going to do next season. No other sponsorships have come through and I am getting nervous. I still have the rubber band on my wrist and I start to snap it.

"Helio, I know how you feel," Adilson tells me. "We are immigrant kids. We are far from home, far from our families. It is harder for us, but we cannot accept failure. You cannot just give up on the dream. You have to find another way. There is always another way."

The rest of the day I think about his words. I turn them over and over in my head and try to come up with "another way." Then it comes to me.

I call Steve Horne and propose that we make a deal. "Listen," I say, "I will win five races and you can keep the prize money until I pay you back. I will drive for free, as long as I can drive. And I know I can win five races."

"I know you can, too," Steve tells me. "It's a deal."

I win the pole position at the first race in Homestead, Florida, but I don't place. At the second race I win the pole position again and this time I place in first. I make my first payment back to the team. I am not collecting any winnings for myself, so in mid-April I am still squatting in the Miami house.

Then a minor miracle occurs.

I am lounging on the couch, watching TV, when the phone rings. I have given out the number to a few people in case of an emergency, so I debate if I should answer it or not. I am worried that it might be the president of Hudson. I pick it up and hesitantly say, "Hello?"

"Hello, Helio. This is Emerson."

"Emerson? Emerson who?"

"Emerson Fittipaldi."

What? This is the guy I worshipped growing up and now he is on the other end of the phone line? "Hello," I say, trying to sound casual. "Can you hold a moment?"

This is like Michael Jordan calling up a high school basketball player. I stand up from the couch and try to calm myself. I position myself in the middle of the Oriental rug. I clear my throat, throw my shoulders back, and take a stance I deem appropriate for talking to a man like Emerson Fittipaldi. I lift the phone to my ear.

"Hello, Emerson."

"Helio, I have been following your career. I am very impressed. You are very talented and I would like to represent you."

I stay silent.

"You would not have to worry about finding sponsors or

anything like that. I will take care of everything for you. You just drive."

I take the phone from my ear and stare at the receiver. This cannot be real. "Helio," he says again, "I would like to represent you. Would you be interested?"

"Yes," I stammer. "Yes, of course."

After we hang up, I immediately call my family. "You will not believe what just happened." I can barely get it out.

I replay the entire conversation. They are beside themselves with happiness. For me, it is an incredible daydream. For all of us, it is the grandest miracle imaginable, the answer to all of our prayers.

My father no longer has to put up money, Kati no longer has to look for sponsors, and the family can now focus on making my father's business profitable again. This is the big break we have been working for since I was eleven. Finally, we can all breathe a sigh of relief.

I sign with Emerson in June. He asks me to meet him at Capital Grille, a steakhouse in Miami. "I thought you didn't eat red meat," I say.

"No, I eat red meat. Do you?"

"Oh no, but don't worry about me. I'll find something." I don't tell him that I have not eaten red meat in eight years because of his 1989 post-Indy interview. I sit around the table with Emerson, his son, and two of his business executives. All of them order big, juicy steaks. I think I am the only one in the whole restaurant who orders chicken. As Emerson begins to tell stories, he waves his hands around and I notice the Indy ring on his right ring finger. He is funny and really knows how to tell a story. I like him at once. A few people have warned me to be careful, because he has a reputation of being a bit hot-tempered and calculating, but I don't see any evidence of that. He tells me that he will bring me to the next level and I will never have to worry about the money side of the business again. It is all I ever wanted. It is a dream come true.

Emerson comes on as my manager for the remainder of the 1997 season and takes me under his wing. I am driving very well and placing in almost every race. He brings me to parties and I feel that I have joined the top ranks. He knows everybody in the racing world and his name opens all doors. I am both impressed and intrigued by his level of fame.

After the final race, on September 27, I go home to Brazil to be with my family. For once we do not have to spend the first weeks of the off-season trying to find a ride and scrounging for sponsors. Emerson is taking care of that now. November passes and there is still no word about a ride; however, I am not worried. After all, I am now being managed by the great Emerson Fittipaldi. What can go wrong? Christmas comes and still, no word of a ride. "Don't worry," Emerson keeps telling me. "Everything is under control."

"I am not worried," I say.

One night, Emerson takes me out to a wild party at a mansion in São Paulo. His level of fame in Brazil is inconceivable. When we walk into the party, everyone turns. I am the youngest person there and it is definitely a different crowd than I am used to hanging around. I discover that an entirely different league of women are approaching me—and I am sure it's because I walked in with Emerson. After about an hour, I am uncomfortable in the house. I cannot find Emerson and I don't know anybody else there. This feels like a moment when I have a choice to make. Do I stay and drink and take advantage of my pseudo-celebrity status? Or do I go home so that I can get up early for a run? I walk through the house still looking for Emerson and I see that none of the people here is having that same internal debate. When I step into the kitchen a group is gathered around the counter; in the center is a pile of white powder. It is the first time I have seen hard drugs. Okay, I think, this is not my kind of party. I call a cab and am happy to go home and get to bed. The next morning, I wake up at six for a run and head to the track.

I am finding myself in these situations more and more often, and I see how easy it could be to travel down the wrong path. One wrong decision and it all goes up in smoke. The drugs and the women are always around and I know I have a choice to make. I choose racing. I choose 6 a.m. runs and 7 a.m. practice laps. The women will come later, I reason. When I make it to the top, the women will come. For now I want to focus on being the best.

After Christmas, Kati and I go to Rio to spend New Year's with some friends. On January 2 I get a call from Emerson's office manager. "We got you a test with Bettenhausen Racing. You will be the only one they are testing," he tells me. As soon as I hang up, I tell Kati and my friends and they start screaming and celebrating. We raise our glasses: "To 1998, the year that everything is going to fall into place."

We drive back to São Paulo the next day and I fly to Miami to test. I sign with Bettenhausen. Emerson guarantees that he will find $1 million in sponsorships for the team, while the main sponsor for Bettenhausen, Alumax, provides the other $6 million. A few months after I sign, Emerson calls Kati and says he has been having trouble finding sponsors. "I thought it would be easier," he tells her. "Would you be able to help me?"

Kati agrees, proud that Emerson wants her assistance. She and my father find $1 million in sponsorship money from Consul, a Brazilian company similar to Whirlpool in the United States. In addition, Emerson secures another $1 million from the Ericsson cell phone company. Things are looking good—we have more than covered the sponsorship requirement for the season.

My first race in IndyCar is at Homestead in Miami, 1998. I am practicing before the race when one of the shocks on the car breaks. I fly into the wall at 193 g's (193 times the weight of my body). When I get out of the car, my head is throbbing, but the only part that scares me is the possibility that I will not be allowed to race. I know that the officials will not allow it if they suspect I have a concussion. I ask my doctor, "What are they going to ask to make sure I don't have a concussion?"

"They will usually ask for your name, if you are okay, and where you are," he tells me.

I practice. "My name is Helio Castroneves. I am fine. I am in Homestead. My name is Helio Castroneves. I am fine. I am in Homestead." I drill it into my concussed head. When they ask me the standard questions, I answer them like a robot. "My name is Helio Castroneves . . ." It works and they clear me for racing.

For every race after this one, I decide that I will memorize the answers to the concussion questions: My name is Helio Castroneves. I am fine. I am in Detroit. I am in Vancouver. I am in Long Beach.

Nineteen ninety-eight proves to be a good year. Emerson takes care of me financially and coaches me, sharing his experiences and giving me tips and tricks for each track. My family doesn't have to worry about me. They can stay in Brazil and focus on my father's company. And for the first time in my adult life, I am able to pay my own rent.

ſ

In the middle of 1999, because of money issues, things take a turn. Alumax, Bettenhausen's main sponsor, is bought

out by another company. As a result they end their relationship with Bettenhausen. We still have another half
a season to find me a team for next year; however, even
though Emerson is aware of the problem, he doesn't take
action right away. "Don't worry," he tells me. "Everything is
under control."

We get a call from the Chip Ganassi Team, one of the best
in the IndyCar Series. Their driver, Alex Zanardi, is going
to Formula One so they have an open seat for testing. Best
of all, no sponsorship money is required. The Chip Ganassi
Team will cover everything. It is perfect! Emerson says no.
The Ganassi team uses a Honda engine and Emerson is
insistent that we stay with a Mercedes engine.

"Emerson," I say, "it doesn't matter to me what kind of
engine we have, as long as I have a seat and we don't have to
look for sponsors. And this is a *good* seat."

"No, we have to stick with a Mercedes engine. It is the better engine."

But that year I have entered twenty-two races and, between
qualifying, practicing, and racing, my engine has blown
thirty-five times. "Maybe it is time to try a different kind of
engine," I say.

"No." Emerson holds firm. "A team with a Mercedes
engine will come through." Juan Pablo Montoya, my old
friend from our go-karting days, takes the seat. I am feeling
terrible. I don't have a team for next year and I don't agree
with any of Emerson's decisions. But he is my manager and
I have to trust him. The only thing for me to do is hope for
another opportunity. A few weeks later, Bobby Rahal's team
approaches me. It is one of the best teams in IRL and I am
sure that Emerson will let me test with them, but again he
says no because of their engine. I am incredibly frustrated
but try to keep my mouth shut and focus on my driving.

Then I get a third break. J. J. Lehto, a driver for Team Hogan, has been fired for some reason and this provides a late opening. I go to speak with Carl Hogan and we immediately take a liking to one another. Hogan agrees to sign me, under the condition that we raise at least $3 million. "No problem," Emerson says. "I will guarantee one million dollars before the season starts and then we will pay out the other two million over the season." I am relieved. Everything is put in order. Emerson will take care of the business side and I will focus on driving.

"Helio," Emerson says, "if I am going to find one million dollars, I need a guarantee from you. I will sign these contracts with Hogan if you sign a five-year extension on my management contract."

I am conflicted. At this point my father has been telling me that Emerson is not doing his job. He is also taking his 20 percent manager's commission from any sponsorships that Kati has found, without giving her a cut. My father tries to make me see that Emerson is taking advantage of me. We have many heated discussions over it. I tell my father that he's wrong. I insist that he doesn't know what he is talking about and that Emerson has been doing all that he can. I am young, perhaps a bit naïve, and Emerson is my childhood idol. I don't want to believe what my father is telling me. I hastily put my signature on the papers and don't tell my father right away since I suspect he won't be happy about it.

In the middle of the season, my boss, Carl Hogan, calls me. "If Emerson doesn't come up with the money," he says, "we will have to let you go."

I am confused. "What do you mean? He has not paid you yet?"

"No." He explains that Emerson has not secured any of the $3 million in sponsorships, and because of this, the team is forced to withhold my salary. I try calling Emerson but can't get through to him. I am growing frustrated and disillusioned. He has been mostly absent the whole year, only showing up for one or two races. Now I can't even get him on the phone. He is promoting a race in Rio and I am starting to feel like his first priority has become finding sponsorship for that event and not for me. Has my father been right all along?

When I finally reach Emerson I ask him what is going on. "Don't worry," he says. "It is under control. We have lots of sponsors."

"Okay," I say, wanting to believe him. I remain focused on driving and expect he will take care of the money. He is still not showing up to my races and I travel alone for most of that season, using my savings from the year before to make my travel arrangements. I am not yet receiving a salary, because Emerson has not yet found any sponsors. I am running out of funds and using my rent money in order to travel to the races.

Hogan calls me into his office one day. "Listen, I understand what is going on here," he says. "Emerson has still not produced the sponsor money, but you are doing an incredible job. I am going to advance your salary out of my own pocket." Carl is frustrated, because paying me means that Emerson is still going to take his 20 percent cut. He will be paying a guy who owes him $3 million and I can see that it makes him furious. However, if he doesn't advance my pay, I will not have had the money to even travel to the races. He is stuck, and because he is such a nice man, he wants to help me out.

At this point I have not seen Emerson for a few months. When we speak on the phone, he only repeats his mantra, "Don't worry. It is under control." I am booking my own tickets and arranging my schedule. It becomes overwhelming and I tell Kati I can't manage everything on my own. I need help.

"But what is Emerson doing?" she asks. "Isn't this his job? He is charging twenty percent of your earnings and doing no work. He is taking advantage of you."

"Can you help me?" I ask her. I don't want to defend Emerson any longer, because I suspect she is right. She moves in with me and starts to take care of all the things that Emerson has neglected.

My family begins to pressure me. "This is not right! He is not doing his job." Now I have to tell them that I cannot fire him because I signed an extension with him. My father goes ballistic. "How could you do this? We have been behind you from the start. I have spent all of my money and all of my time on you. How could you compromise me like this?" I don't know what to say. I know he's right and I've never felt worse.

I have had several offers from top teams throughout the year. I wonder how different my season would have been if we had accepted the offer from the Chip Ganassi Team— Juan Pablo Montoya is leading the series and I cannot help but think I could have been in that position, in that car. And I wouldn't be worrying about these money issues. Though my own team is underfunded, we are still racing well. However, every time I take the lead in a race, my engines seems to fail. Maybe this is a sign? Emerson keeps telling me not to worry, that everything will work out, but I have serious doubts. I begin to realize that though Emerson was a great driver, he is not a good manager.

The final race of the year is held on October 31 in Fontana, California. Once again Emerson doesn't show up. Kati is there, and though they are angry with me about signing that extension, my parents have flown in from Brazil. The night before the race, Carl Hogan calls me to his office. He sits me down, along with the team manager, and explains that he is shutting down his team. "Helio," he says, "all season long Emerson has paid me in promises. I cannot pay my bills with promises. I think you are an incredible talent and you have a bright future, but Emerson will not take you any farther. I have to pay my bills and I can't put my company, the family company, in jeopardy. So, I am not happy about it, but that is why I am closing the team." I think about Hogan's words: "I cannot put my company, the family company, in jeopardy." Suddenly it strikes me that that is exactly what my father did for me.

I keep trying to call Emerson, but he doesn't answer. At last I get ahold of him. "Where are you?" I ask. "We have a major problem. Hogan is not having a team next year. I don't have a ride . . ."

"Don't worry," he tells me. "I have a sponsor that is going to give us twenty million dollars to form a Brazilian team for next year!"

"Don't tell me not to worry!" I yell. "You could not find a million dollars and now you say you have twenty million? Come on! I'm not stupid."

He doesn't say anything.

For once I speak my mind. "Again, I am without a ride. You didn't do what you were supposed to do! And now you aren't even here on the last race!"

"Yes, but I sent my son-in-law. He is there to help you."

"Your son-in-law can't help me! I need my manager here! What am I supposed to do now?"

He doesn't say anything to that. I can tell by the background noise that he's on his boat and this makes me even angrier. I try to calm myself. "You didn't come to my races," I tell him. "You didn't find sponsors, you made Carl upset, you turned down two other teams that offered me a ride, and now I don't have a team for next year. This is not working. I have to end this relationship. I no longer need you to speak on my behalf."

He doesn't seem upset and only says, "Okay, fine then." When I hang up, I feel desperate and disillusioned. I realize that I'm on my own now and I hope that my family will forgive me for my mistakes.

I go out to dinner with Kati and my parents and tell them what has happened. I apologize for signing the extension, I apologize for wasting the family's money, and I apologize for my failure. "I've released Emerson as my manager," I say, "but I think it's too late. I think this is the end of the road."

"No," my father tells me. "We don't swim across the entire ocean to die fifty feet from the shore."

Kati is determined. "Let's go to every team. We will knock on every door. We will find you a ride."

"We will figure something out," my mother assures me. "We are here for you."

And so, abandoned by my childhood hero, I fall once again into the arms of my family. We have twenty-four hours to find me a ride; otherwise my U.S. work visa will be terminated and we'll all be headed back to Brazil.

CHAPTER 5

Summoned to the Pits

**None of us knows what might happen
even the next minute, yet still we go
forward. Because we trust.
Because we have Faith.**

—PAULO COELHO

I WAKE UP THE morning of October 31, 1999, desperate and depressed—a twenty-four-year-old washout. It's the standard Brazilian race car driver's story: a family bankrupt, a dream deferred, a father helpless, a mother left gripping her rosary. And then there is Kati: a sister who has given up her ambitions to help her brother pursue his.

Where do I go from here? I have no education, no savings, no marketable skill. I don't know how to properly fix an engine or change a tire or check the oil. I am a race car driver who cannot even be a mechanic. All I know is how to hold a steering wheel and drive. Since the time I was eleven, everything has been secondary to racing.

As the years passed by, and as the family money depleted, holding that steering wheel grew from a boyhood dream to a family dream. It grew from a family dream to a Castroneves business venture. And then it became the Castroneves family's only hope. If there was a backup plan, it would have been for me to work at my father's company, but now that too is gone. The future of my family lands squarely upon my shoulders and I can no longer carry the burden.

I want to scream at them, "I did not ask for this! I did not ask for a publicist at eleven years old. I did not ask for Kati to drop out of her ballet company, to sell her apartment, and to live on her friends' couches. I did not ask

Dad to sell all of his properties, to take out loans, or to go into such severe debt. I did not ask for everyone to bank everything on me!" But of course, I don't say any of this, because a part of me wonders if I did in fact ask for this. Was this all my doing?

∫

We stand together, a desperate foursome, at a racetrack in Fontana, California, on a sunny October morning.

I can feel my parents' panic. My father remains silent and solemn. My mother shifts her eyes, her feet, her whole body from side. They don't offer up the familiar chant: *Focus, go forward, just drive.* The only words I hear are those of my mother softly praying the rosary as she holds the beads in her tight knuckles.

Kati stands next to me, grabs my hands, and squeezes. "Don't worry, Helio," she tells me. "Focus on the race. It will be fine. Something will work out." She smiles and I can see that she is confident that it will all work out, though I don't know how.

Before the race, Kati goes from team to team, knocking on the trailer doors, asking to speak to them. I go with her to see Bobby Rahal, one of the owners whom Emerson had turned away during the season. "I'm sorry," he says, "but we've already found a new driver." I am in panic mode. For the first time I begin to really worry about the business side of things. The little English I know has abandoned me. I don't understand what anyone is saying. Kati explains to me that every team has filled its seats, but there is still one possibility, Walker Racing.

Walker Racing provides a small ray of hope. Their driver, Gil de Ferran, is going to Penske Racing and his seat is available. Kati and I go to see Derrick Walker, the team owner, and his attorney, Alan Miller. This is the first time I have met Alan Miller, though I have heard a lot about him. He is a former NFL football player who is now one of the best sports attorneys. He has represented most of the best drivers and I can see he's willing to help me out in any way he can. However, he is not able to represent me because he is already representing Walker Racing. "You have to find yourself an attorney," he informs me. "You have to protect yourself." I begin to wonder if I was supposed to have had an attorney this whole time.

101

Derrick Walker explains the situation to Kati and me: "We have a ride, but you will need to come up with the sponsor money." Not only that, but Carl Hogan owns my option and we'll have to buy him out for $1 million. We'll also have to pay back Emerson's $3 million debt to the Hogan team. Everyone is trying to come up with solutions, not just for me, but also for Carl Hogan. Nobody wants to see his team fold. However, it soon becomes clear that there is nothing to be done. It is an impossible situation. Our hope dies as quickly as it was ignited. This is the end of the line—a heartbreaking final chapter to a long, frustrating saga.

I head to the infield for one last race—the Marlboro 500. I have five hundred miles and two hundred and fifty laps left in my career. Five hundred miles and half that many laps until my life will shift forever. I step into my car, grab the steering wheel, and breathe deeply. I feel as I always feel when I grab a steering wheel: in control. Despite all that has occurred over the past twenty-four hours and all the uncertainty that lies before me, in my car at this very moment, I am calm.

I start in seventeenth place and quickly move up to fourth. I block out all the turmoil and focus on what is immediately ahead. Then, just ten laps into the race, as I am pressing forward, I see a car go out of control in front of me. It hurls toward the infield wall at over two hundred miles an hour. I fly by, unsure of what has just happened.

In the pits, my parents and Kati stand, shocked and paralyzed. They have seen the horrifying crash in its entirety. Greg Moore, the brightest up-and-coming star in CART racing, spun out, hit an access road, flipped upside down, and then slammed into the concrete wall at 240 miles an hour. The car rolled over several times, breaking apart, until it settled on the infield grass, leaving everyone stunned and sickened. Fear grips the crowd. The race has only just begun and that unwelcome reminder of danger and death has entered the stadium.

Yet none of the drivers knows any of this. The race continues. I see that there is a commotion near the part of the track where the car flipped, but I don't allow myself to look. I have been trained never to look, to never let a speck of fear or distraction enter my mind.

About a hundred laps into the race, my car suffers a mechanical failure and I have to pull out. When I get to the pits, the rest of the team tells me that Greg has been airlifted to a nearby medical center and despite many efforts to revive him, he has died from massive head injuries. The race has not yet ended, but the track flags are already flying at half-staff. My God, I think, this just gets worse and worse.

I walk to my trailer to change. Once I am alone, I mourn the loss of a colleague and the end of my career.

There are no victory celebrations after the race; instead there are makeshift memorial services. People wander around too stunned to speak. Greg Moore was a mere twenty-four years old and had just signed a multiyear deal with Penske, the top team in the league. He was expected to be one of the greatest drivers the sport had ever seen, deemed the future of IndyCar. There was no telling how high his star would rise. Above all, he was an extraordinary guy, capable of being the fiercest competitor on the track and the sociable compatriot off the track. He was a fan favorite and everyone's friend. It is an enormous and heartbreaking loss.

I find my parents and my sister. Nobody can talk. My mother cannot stop crying. We all are thinking what we will never say: That could have been me. The memorial service ends and the track begins to empty. I go back to my trailer. I don't know what to do with myself. Fear and trepidation grip me. I realize that my U.S. work visa will now be terminated. I am headed back to Brazil with my family, with no money and no hope for a future. I have mixed feelings. Though I don't have a ride, I am safe and alive. I sit on the floor of my trailer and hold my head in my hands. Then I hear a knock at the door. "Come in," I call. The door opens and Dan Luginbuhl, vice president of the Penske Corporation, stands in front of me. "Roger Penske would like to see you in the pit lane," he says. "Can you be there in fifteen minutes?"

"Yes," I say, and then wait a long fifteen minutes before I walk to the pit lane. Nobody is there. It is dusk and I stand alone, watching the sun set in the California sky. A few minutes later, a white car comes over the horizon. It is Roger Penske and his son, Greg Penske, the president of Penske Motorsports. The car stops in front of me and Roger holds out his hand to introduce himself, "Hello, Helio," he says. "Please, get in."

I sit in the backseat and as we drive away, we make small

talk. I am a bit shell-shocked and unsure of what to say in the situation. The flags around the track are still flying at half-staff. The grief is still palpable. Yet, here I am, in the backseat of Roger Penske's car, with the most successful owner of the most successful team in all of racing. We pass the accident scene. "Such a shame," Roger says. We all nod. "We have to do something here. We have to make it safer." Nobody says anything for a few moments. When we arrive at the track exit Roger turns around to look at me. "Helio, can you be in the Doubletree Hotel at seven-forty-five? The presidential suite? We have to talk."

"Yes," I say, nodding my head.

I get out of the car and walk off to find my family. They are waiting in our hotel across the highway from the Doubletree and I tell them that I am going to meet Roger Penske at 7:45. None of us dares to get our hopes up. "Kati," I say, "you have to come with me." I can't speak English well enough, and Kati can speak a little more than I, though not by much. Together, I figure we might be able to keep up with the conversation. At seven-thirty, Kati and I walk across the highway. Our parents stay behind in the hotel room, waiting.

When we walk into the presidential suite, we see Roger and Greg Penske sitting at a conference table along with several other men. We are introduced to Roger's attorneys, then to Tim Cindric, the president of Penske Racing. And finally to Gil de Ferran, a well-known Brazilian race car driver who, along with Greg Moore, has just signed a multi-year agreement with Penske.

At first they think Kati is my girlfriend, but we explain that she is my sister and is here to help me with the English. We sit down at the table and Gil gets up and makes his way to the door. As he passes by he whispers to me in Portuguese, "Just follow his lead."

After he leaves, Roger begins to talk. "This is a very difficult time. We are deeply saddened by what has happened this afternoon. But life goes on. Racing goes on. Our main sponsor, Marlboro, requires that we have a driver set in place by Thursday. And not just any driver, a top driver. We would like to know if you are interested."

Instinctively I say, "Yes." Then I pause.

"Who is your attorney?" he asks. "Who is your manager?"

"I don't have either."

"Okay, I will give you time to find an attorney and we can go from there. But we need an answer by the end of the week."

I am happy and excited, of course, but I am also conflicted. I cannot really think straight. I certainly don't want to replace anyone under these conditions, but I don't want to go back to Brazil, either. The range of emotions in one day is too overwhelming to process. Stripped of a ride, abandoned by my childhood idol, witness to the death of a peer, and now asked to drive for the greatest team in racing.

We decide to stay in California that night and leave for Miami the next morning to find an attorney. We call the only lawyer we know, my friend Mark Seidon, who once helped me get out of a speeding ticket. "We need you to help us find a lawyer," I say.

"What about Alan Miller? He is the biggest race car drivers' lawyer." But Alan was also Greg Moore's attorney. We are not sure if it would be a conflict of interest. I call him that afternoon and after I explain my situation, he agrees to represent me. The first thing he tells me to do is send a formal letter to Emerson terminating our business relationship. He explains that since Emerson has not met his commitments, the contract is null and void.

Then we begin to talk to Penske. When it comes time to establish a salary, Roger asks me, "What do you think you are worth?"

"I don't know," I say. "I have no idea. Alan mentioned I should get two million."

"Okay, two million it is."

I cannot believe it. I would have raced for Penske for free!

On Thursday, we are scheduled to fly to Detroit to meet with Alan and Roger. Kati and I ask Mark to accompany us. "You have to come," we tell him. "We need you to read the contracts. Our English is not good enough." He agrees and the three of us arrive in Detroit late on Thursday night. Mark picks up a packet of contracts about six inches thick and we all sit in my hotel room as he begins to go through them.

Alan had been negotiating Greg Moore's contract with Penske for months. The contracts were so involved because Alan was making sure that Greg was covered from every angle—health insurance, life insurance, a retirement plan. They used the same blueprint for me, and cut and pasted my name for Greg Moore's. For the first time in my racing career, I have health insurance! But that is not the most exciting part of the contract for me. The part I am most interested in concerns the number of years Penske is signing me for.

"What does it say?" Kati and I keep asking. "Does it say three years?"

Mark scans the documents. "Yes. Three years. You are guaranteed a ride for three years."

"Oh my God, three years! Three years!"

For me, "three years" are the two most important words in that contract. I would have signed it for free, as long as I was assured that I would be racing for three straight seasons.

We keep jumping on the bed and screaming, "Three years!" until Mark finally says, "Guys, I can't read these if you don't shut up."

"Oh, let's read them in the morning," we say. "It's too late. We've been traveling all day. Let's go to bed and we can wake up early to go through them." We are meeting Roger at ten the next morning at the Dearborn Inn, so there should be enough time.

But our alarms never go off and we all wake up at 10:45. We frantically rush out of our hotel and, of course, Mark never has time to read the rest of the contracts. No matter. He read the important parts. Penske Racing. Three years. Two million dollars per year.

ſ

Kati, Mark Seidon, and I rush through the lobby. Roger Penske is waiting in the boardroom with his attorney, Larry Bluth; my attorney, Alan Miller; and the vice president of Penske Corporation, Dan Luginbuhl. We begin to shake hands all around.

"I'm sorry we're late," I say. "But I want to tell you that we are really excited."

"We are excited, as well," Roger tells us. When we are finished shaking hands with everyone, we sit down and Roger says, "So, are we all set to sign?"

"Yes, I am all set."

We sit down at the boardroom table and pages of contracts start to shift in front of me. Pages are flipped and fingers point to the lines where I should sign. "Sign here, and here, and here." Flip, flip, flip. "Now sign here, and here, and here." The entire matter takes about an hour.

After all the contracts and forms are signed, Luginbuhl tells me he'll be in touch to give me all the phone numbers and information I will need.

"Thank you," I say to him. Kati, Mark, and I walk back out into the cool fall air. We look at each other. Now what? Alan Miller has invited us to his home to see his new baby.

We fly back to Miami that night. Adilson Rodrigues has left me a few messages. A year ago, I had recommended that Emerson hire him as his landscaper. Now Emerson is frantically calling him, demanding to know where I am. "Man, Emerson is freaking out," Adilson's messages say. "He keeps asking me where you are. He is going to kill me!"

I call Adilson back. "Don't worry," I say. "I'm going to talk to him."

"Just so you know, he is really mad. Be careful."

"Okay, thanks."

A few days later, I have my first formal meeting with Alan Miller. He starts to explain to me how payment is going to work. "So," he says, "all payments will be made to your company, Seven Promotions."

"Wait—Seven Promotions is not my company," I tell him.

"What do you mean? Who owns it?"

"I don't know."

Alan looks nervous. He has used the same template for my contract as he did for Greg Moore's, just crossing out Greg's name and penciling in mine. His secretary has also crossed out Greg's company name, Greg Moore Enterprises, and replaced it with Seven Promotions. The problem now is that Greg owned Greg Moore Enterprises. I don't own Seven. The issue is compounded by the fact that Greg was a Canadian citizen living in Canada. I am a Brazilian citizen living in America. Our tax requirements are completely different. Because the contracts has been so rushed, we have never discussed any of this before the signing.

"Helio," Alan says, "all the contracts you signed with Penske state that your payment be made to this company, Seven Promotions. And you don't know who owns it?"

"No."

"When I asked you if you had a company, you told me Seven."

"I'm sorry. I didn't understand. I thought you needed a company so that I could sign the contracts. I thought that was how Penske worked."

"And so why did you tell me Seven?"

"Because my father had told me last year that this company, Seven, was going to be used to help protect my finances. He and Kati had found sponsors and he didn't want Emerson to take the commission."

"So your father owns Seven?"

"I am not sure."

Alan looks nervous. He picks up the phone and calls Larry Bluth, Penske's attorney. "Don't make any payments to Seven," Alan tells Larry. "I am not sure who owns it, but it's not Helio's company."

I walk out of Alan's office after the phone call and am certain that it will all be figured out. I don't give the conversation a second thought. I just want to race.

ſ

A week later, I go back Brazil. I have decided that I should meet with Emerson face-to-face. I want to clear the air and make sure there are no hard feelings.

"I will go with you," my father says as I leave for Emerson's office in São Paulo.

"No, I have to do this by myself," I tell him. "I got myself into this. I can get myself out."

I drive the hundred and fifty miles from Ribeirão Preto to São Paulo, preparing what I have to say to him.

When I walk into Emerson's office, he is sitting in a chair, nervous and agitated. The letter of termination I have sent him sits on his desk. "I know that this was a mistake," he begins. "You were upset. Don't worry. We can forget all about it."

"No, Emerson, it wasn't a mistake. It was very deliberate."

The blood rushes to his face. His smiles fades into a scowl and his dark eyes turn cold. "Why would you do this to me?"

"Because, Emerson, I told you many times that we should try new avenues. I should have tested with Bobby Rahal when he asked me. I should have tested with Chip Ganassi when they asked me. I could have driven for both of them without having to find sponsors."

"I told you . . ." He tries to cut me off, but for the first time in my life, I take control outside of the race car.

"You told me that you had sponsors, but you never did. You told me that everything would be okay, but then I was left without a team because you never paid Hogan. I had no choice. If I don't take care of my career, nobody will."

He begins to scream. "You cannot do this to me! You cannot do this to me!" He pounds the desk with his fist over and over.

"I'm sorry. It is not that I cannot do it. It is done."

"I am going to sue you!" He continues to scream and pound at the desk. He is a man possessed and I am starting to get scared.

The security guards rush in. "What's going on?"

"He's crazy," I tell them. "I'm out of here."

When I get in my car, I let out a sigh of relief. I feel as

though I have just ended a bad relationship that should have been walked away from long ago. I feel free. I drive to the airport, eager to get back to America, back to the track.

The plane takes off, São Paulo for Miami. I close my eyes, inhale deeply, and smile, ready to start a new chapter.

Part 2

**All I had to do was
keep turning left.**

—GEORGE ROBSON,
WINNER OF 1946 INDY 500

CHAPTER 6

180 Degrees

**When you want something,
all the universe conspires
in helping you achieve it.**
—PAULO COELHO

On January 2, 2000, a box arrives at the doorstep of my Miami apartment. Inside is my new red Marlboro racing suit from Team Penske.

"Kati," I call. "Kati, come look."

"What?" She walks in the room and pauses when she sees it. "Oh my God! Try it on! Try it on!"

I step into the suit, button it up to my neck, and look to Kati.

"How do I look?"

"You look like a champion."

In Brazil, the red Marlboro suit is legendary. It carries the weight of history and success. When we think of champion drivers, we think of them in red from head to foot, a white-and-black Marlboro patch on the left chest.

I walk over to my full-length mirror and start to turn, inspecting myself from all angles. MARLBORO is written in big black letters across my stomach. My chest and sleeves are peppered with the logos of my sponsors—Mobil, Honda, Hugo Boss, and others. Sponsors that I didn't have to worry about finding! And on the top-left shoulder is the white insignia of Penske Racing. I strike a pose, lift my hands over my head, and imagine myself winning my first race, winning the Indianapolis 500, winning the championship. And then I imagine myself at fourteen years old, in my all-red Corpal racing suit that my father and I had designed to emulate this one. I think of myself as a fourteen-year-old boy on the racetracks of São Paulo, winning my first trophy and wishing for the day that I would be wearing the real Marlboro suit. Ten years later, the dream has crystallized into reality.

∫

118

Later that week I have my first practice with Team Penske at Sebring Raceway. It is a two-hour drive from my apartment and on the way there, I am singing, banging the steering wheel, happy to get back on the track. I meet with Tim Cindric, this time under less stressful circumstances. He explains that he will be my race strategist and Roger will be the race strategist for Gil de Ferran.

The relationship with my strategist is crucial since he is the guy speaking in my ear during every race. It is essential that we connect, but on the surface it seems Cindric and I have nothing in common. Tim is a tall, blond-haired, blue-eyed guy from Indiana. He's an all-American fellow with a cool demeanor and a college education. I am a short, dark-haired, dark-eyed immigrant from Brazil. I have a hyperactive personality, very poor English skills, and my only education has been on the racetrack. But we have a few key things in common. We have the same viewpoint on racing, we have a similar sense of humor, and we started our careers with Penske together. The tragic Greg Moore race was Cindric's first race with Penske, so this is the rookie season for both of us.

Most important, Cindric somehow understands my English. And I can somehow understand his (perhaps because he knows to speak to me in all-racing terms). After the first few minutes together, we become fast friends.

Cindric introduces me to the team. My head engineer

is Andy Borme, who was with me in 1996, '97, and '99 with Hogan. Because the engineer acts as the interpreter between the driver and the car, it is very important to connect with them as well. I am happy that I have somebody I have worked with before.

When I see the car—red and white with the same Penske and Marlboro labels that are on my racing suit—I am anxious get in and run. This car, like the racing suit, is legendary in Brazil. It is like the New York Yankees uniform in America.

We spend the beginning of the day setting up the car, fitting it to my body and my style. It is like altering clothes—no two guys are going to have exactly the same suit measurements and no two guys are going to have the same race car settings. There are many adjustments that have to be made to make a car more aerodynamic for each driver. When the car has been set up to fit my body and driving style, I start to run a few laps. I can feel the difference in the car right away. I am flying, clocking in the fifties. In the past I was always clocking in the fifty-ones and fifty-twos.

When I get home, I tell Kati, "You have to see the car. It's amazing. It flies." I go on an on, describing the two-day practice to her.

When I am finished she says, "Awesome! This is going to be your year. I can feel it."

I hope so. Up until now, my racing career has been a bit of a roller coaster. The past few years have been full of roadblocks—sponsors falling through, my team folding, my father falling into bankruptcy, all the problems with Emerson—but now I feel like the path is clearing. This really could be my year.

"By the way, Helio," Kati says, "do you know how I should send an invoice?"

"An invoice? No. For what?"

"The manager at Penske said I should fax him an invoice every time you practice or travel and that kind of thing." For us, this is new territory. But then again, everything is new. We have never had a company before. We have to learn how to send an invoice, buy fax machines and office supplies, and most important, find a place to start an office. We begin from scratch.

I also discover that it is time to have my own space.

Kati tells me one night, "I invited a guy over for dinner tonight."

"What? No, no, no." I hold my hand up. "This is my apartment. No guys."

"It's my apartment, too."

"No guys."

"Okay, Helio. Whatever you say." She is not happy about it, but come on! I have to protect my sister (plus, I really do want to relax).

A few days later, I invite a girl over and Kati holds her hand up to me. "No, no, no. No girls."

"Okay," I say. "I think it's time we found you a separate apartment."

"Sounds like a good idea."

When my mom finds out, she calls us up crying. "You are supposed to stick together," she says.

"We are. But we don't need to spend every second with each other. We eat together, work together, travel together. We need our own space."

"But you are brother and sister."

Mom cannot understand. In Brazil it is very common to live with your family until you get married. But Kati and I are adapting to the American ways and beginning to understand the logic of not living with your siblings in your midtwenties.

We find her an apartment two buildings down and set up a little makeshift office for the new family company. I still cannot believe how quickly my life has turned. An invisible force has taken hold of me, spun me 180, and I am just trying to regain my footing.

When the season begins, I am listed as Helio Castro Neves, my legal name; however, the reporters and announcers are calling me Helio Castro or Helio Neves, but never my whole name. They keep asking saying, "Helio who?" or "Helio what?" One reporter tells me, "Lose the dash and go fast." By the fourth race of 2000, I take his advice and I am finally called by my full name. From now on, I decide, I will be Helio Castroneves.

Cindric and I are finding our groove and learning how to communicate with each other. We make a few mistakes in the process, but each time we make sure to analyze what went wrong. Each misstep makes us stronger as a team. Cindric is a very smart guy strategy-wise and he also knows how to speak to me. He jokes with me that I only know fifty English words, but it seems to be enough to get us by since Cindric says very little over the radio. Some strategists will talk the whole race long, which I find enormously distracting (though some drivers like that).

With Cindric, sometimes ten or fifteen laps will go by without hearing from him. When he does talk, he says as few words as possible, making the tone of his voice just as important as what he says. He will say, "Save fuel," in three different ways. It can mean, "It would be good to save fuel so we will be in a better position later." It can mean, "You are getting a little low on fuel." Or it can mean, "You are going to run out of fuel!" It all depends on how he says it.

By midseason I am feeling comfortable with the team and the car, but I am still hungry for a win.

At the Detroit Grand Prix on June 18, I break through. I start in third position. I am driving conservatively. My racing buddy, Juan Pablo Montoya, is leading and I am right behind. He pits late, and in the sixty-first lap of the race, he is sidelined because of equipment failure. I take the lead with twenty-three laps to go. "Save fuel," Cindric keeps telling me over the radio. "Be conservative." I hate driving conservatively, but I can tell by the tone of Cindric's voice that he is serious. When there are five laps to go, I am still in the lead. They are the slowest five laps of my life. I see somebody coming up from behind. No, buddy, this is my race.

I hang on for the final five laps and capture my first win with Penske. As soon as I cross the finish line, I want to bust out of the car. I have been waiting so long for this day. I hear Cindric yelling in my radio, "Now they are going to know your name, buddy!" I am screaming and crying. I don't know what to do. I just want get out of the car and jump around. I am supposed to drive to the pits, where everybody, including the TV crews, is waiting for me. But I stop in the wrong place and unbuckle myself. The car is practically still rolling as I jump out and start running. I pause in the middle of the infield and look around. Where is everybody? I see the crowd is going crazy and I just want to get near them. I run over to them and, without thinking, I jump up on the fence and start to climb. The crowd goes wild. After that, my entire team comes running and we all celebrate together.

As I am walking to the podium, Bobby Rahal, the president of CART at the time, asks me, "What did you do?"

"I know. I'm sorry. I know I'm not supposed to jump out there. It wasn't intentional."

"No," he says. "That was the best thing that could have happened. That's what the fans need."

The next morning I wake up to see the newspapers have

finally gotten my name right. HELIO CASTRONEVES GETS FIRST CART WIN, the headline reads.

Right after the race we have a media day in Chicago. An ESPN reporter, John Kernan, calls me "Spider-Man" during an interview and the nickname catches on almost instantly. The next race, I see a little kid in a Spider-Man outfit, and the fans start calling out to me.

123

I am beginning to feel like I am earning my place. I have not forgotten that I came in this year through chance and tragic circumstances. I am painfully aware that I am taking the place of Greg Moore, a driver thought to be one of the best the sport would ever see. I respect the situation and it is always in the back of my mind. I know that whenever my name is mentioned, his is mentioned as well. I am asked about him in many of the interviews and I always try to honor him when I speak. I want to prove that I deserve to be here. The win at Detroit is my first stepping-stone.

A few weeks later, at a race in Toronto, I capture another pole position, which is especially gratifying since it has just been renamed the "Greg Moore Pole Position." I put the trophy in my office next to a photo of Greg. Yet it is not until September 3, at a race in Vancouver, British Columbia, when I finally feel like I am where I belong.

The race itself is not all that memorable, but what happens after the race I will never forget. I am in the hospitality area and I see Greg Moore's mother, Donna, at the other side of the suite. I want to talk to her, but it is a delicate subject and I want to make sure to choose the right words. Before I can think of what to say, she walks toward me. "Listen," she says, "I've heard a lot of what you have said about Greg in your interviews. I want you to know that what happened was destiny. I don't want you to feel that you are replacing my son. He is where he is supposed to be and you are where you are supposed to be. Somebody had to follow him. And I am happy that it is you."

I feel as though a thousand pounds have been lifted off of my chest. It is one of the most generous gifts anyone has ever given me.

ſ

I come home to Miami to find a letter from the law offices of Steel, Hector, & Davis.

> Dear Helio Castroneves, Jr. I am writing to inform you that I am claiming the sum of $3.3 million from you for the following reasons. . . .

My heart stops.

"Kati, what is this? What does this mean?" She takes the letter and reads.

"I think it means Emerson is suing you for three-point-three million dollars."

"What do we do?" I am panicked.

"You're asking me? I don't know! Call Alan."

I call Alan and tell him, "Emerson has just sent me a letter saying he is suing me for three-point-three million dollars. What do I do?"

"Don't worry. He has no case," he says. "We expected this, didn't we?" It is true (though I'm still shocked). But for months, Roger Penske and Alan have been trying to nego- tiate a deal with Emerson. Roger even flew us both up to Detroit and tried to mediate the situation. Roger met with me first and I said, "I don't want to fight. Let's just work it so that we don't fight." Then he met with Emerson. Afterward he called me. "I'm sorry," he said. "It's just too difficult. I couldn't work anything out with him." I knew that the next logical step was a lawsuit. Still, when you see your name at the top of a legal letter that begins with the phrase "I am claiming the sum of $3.3 million from you" it pretty much freaks you out.

"You have to get an attorney," Alan says. "I can help with the case, but I can't formally represent you because I am a witness." He gives me the name of an attorney in Miami, Larry Stumpf. I go to Larry's office the following week to meet with him. He has on cowboy boots and a huge silver belt buckle, not at all what I pictured a lawyer should look like. But when we start to talk, I can tell that he is smart and knows his stuff, so despite the questionable belt and the footwear, I trust him.

I have to give my first deposition, which is difficult. It makes everything seem very real and very intense. When I leave the office, I am a bit rattled. I cannot believe this is happening. It takes me a day to recover, but I tell myself that I will tackle each obstacle of the lawsuit as it comes. I am not going to let it take over my life. Whenever I speak with Alan or Larry, it shakes me up for a bit, but then I put my focus back on the track, back where I have control.

ʃ

It is the final race of the season. We are at Fontana, almost exactly a year after Greg Moore's crash. Same track, same race. I am in the lead with twenty laps to go, driving 252 miles per hour, when the engine blows up and locks. My car does a 180 and goes flying backward at about 230 miles per hour. I close my eyes and pray. A millisecond later I feel the impact of car against concrete wall. I open my eyes and realize that I have no breath. I try to suck in a small bit of air. Cindric's voice comes over the radio: "Are you okay? Are you okay?" I am unable to answer.

In twenty seconds the medical crew is upon me. "Are you okay? Are you okay?" Still I cannot answer. I take small breaths and only get out small coughs.

"How are you doing?" they keep asking. I stare at the steering wheel, which has been bent into a pretzel shape. "Talk to us, Helio. How are you?"

Finally I can say, "We are in Fontana. I am fine. My name is Helio Castroneves."

"Why weren't you answering?"

"I couldn't breathe."

"What are you feeling?"

"My lower back. It hurts."

I feel them remove me from the car and put a board under my back. My knees and heels burn. As they wheel me away, I look back and see the car. The front is intact, but the rear is shattered from the force. They take me to an ambulance and Kati runs toward me. When she sees me on the stretcher, she starts to cry. She comes in the ambulance alongside me. "Are you okay? Are you okay?" she asks.

"Dammit," I say to her. "I can't believe it. That was a million-dollar race. I was winning. There were twenty laps to go. It was mine!" I am yelling in Portuguese.

The nurse says to Kati, "What's wrong? Does he need something? Is he okay?"

"No, he's fine," Kati tells her. "He's upset about not winning the race. Now I know he's really fine."

The nurse looks at me as if I'm crazy. When we are on our way to the hospital, she asks me, "Can we cut your suit?"

"Yes, but this is my lucky underwear. Don't cut the underwear."

"Well, it's not lucky anymore."

"Yes, it is. I'm here, aren't I?" They cut it anyway. When we get to the hospital, I see that my parents are there. I can tell that they are shaken up. The doctors keep me on the board and start buzzing around me. I tell them, "My knee is hurting. My knee." I am not sure I am using the right word, because nobody is responding. "My knee, my knee," I keep saying over and over. Then, without warning, the doctor checks me for internal bleeding (this is not a pleasant experience, if you know what I mean). "Hey! What was that?" I yell. "I said my knee! My knee!" I point again.

"You are peeing blood. I had to check for internal bleeding."

They have given me morphine, which is starting to make me nauseous. My heel is burning like hell, but I am afraid to say anything for fear they will check me for something else. Hours pass and finally the main doctor comes and starts putting on a glove. I say, "Hey, hey, hey! What are you doing with that glove? I'm not bleeding internally."

"Don't worry. I'm just going to check on your heel and you'll be off this board soon. Maybe five hours." Five hours? He inspects my feet and tells me I have lost all the skin on my left heel. I can't see it because I am strapped to the board, but now I know why it is burning.

"I can't stay on this board anymore," I try to tell anyone who will listen to me. "I have to sit. I can't be lying down."

Roger and Cindric stop by on their way to the year-end banquet. Gil has won the championship and I am pissed that I am missing the party. Kati goes in my place to accept the Greg Moore Legacy Award on my behalf, "given to a driver who most typifies Moore's distinctive combination of on-track talent and dynamic personality." She comes back to the hospital to show me the award and I tear up. It is one of the most meaningful awards I have ever received.

When the internal bleeding is gone and I am released from the hospital, I walk out bandaged, battered, and bruised. And immensely blessed.

CHAPTER 7

My First Indy

**To finish first,
you must first finish.**

—RICK MEARS

T HE FIRST TIME I see Indianapolis Motor Speedway is in the fall of 2000, when Roger sends me there to test a car. Penske Racing has not entered the Indianapolis 500 since 1995, when American Open Wheel Racing split into two leagues—CART and IRL (Indy Racing League). CART had the better drivers but IRL had the marquee race, the Indy 500. Penske Racing was in the CART league, but Roger was thinking about entering a few IRL races in 2001 so we could race at Indianapolis.

"Listen," Roger tells me, "we might go back to Indy next year. I want you to go out and practice and see how you feel."

When I walk into the speedway, I am impressed by the enormity of the place. I have seen it on TV, of course, but nothing compares to seeing it in person. It is by far the biggest track I have ever been on. A diagram at the entrance boasts that all of the following landmarks would fit within the oval at the same time: Yankee Stadium, the Colosseum in Rome, Vatican City, the Rose Bowl, the All England Lawn and Tennis Croquet Club (better known as Wimbledon), and Churchill Downs.

I remind myself of what Alfredo Guaraná Menezes told me when I first started. "A track is a track. No matter where you are in the world, or how big or intimidating it may look, never forget: A track is a track."

I begin to test the car and I cannot go more than 180, 182. The average pole position is 221. I stop and tell the team, "I think something is wrong with the car."

"No, man, that's just Indy. It's a tough place. Keep going."

I go back out and I am bearing down, pushing as hard as possible, but still that speedometer doesn't go above 184. Something doesn't feel right with the car. I stop again. "I don't know," I tell the guys. "The car is loose." I can see that they're skeptical and think I'm just making excuses. I turn to the head engineer. "I really think something is off. Can you check it out?"

"Okay," he says. "Let's go back to the pad and take a look."

He finds out that the numbers have been faxed over incorrectly. I am relieved. I may be a rookie at Indy, but I know when something is wrong with a car. Still, Indy has earned my respect. They fix the problem and I go back out and start to post 218, 219. There we go. This is more like it. But it is still a tough track to master. The straightaways are very narrow and each of the turns presents a different challenge. It is not an oval, but rather a rectangle, so instead of two turns a lap, there are four. Everything about it is new and exhilarating. I want to know what it will feel like to race on it with a full grandstand.

In 2001, I get my chance. Roger decides that we will race in both leagues—CART and IRL. This means we will be entering twice as many races, which makes me very happy. The countdown to my first 500 begins—May 27, 2001.

After my rookie year with Penske, I have earned two nicknames: Julio (because nobody can say my name right) and Cheapskate (because, well, I was cheap back then). I still have not spent much of the money I have earned during the year. My lawyer has invested it in an account for me and I don't have to worry about it, which is just fine with me. I don't spend much money. I still live in the same apartment, drive the same car, and eat the same rice and chicken mixture I had learned to make in England. I am just very happy to be racing without worrying about sponsors. I have not adopted the crazy South Beach lifestyle, and I am not sure I ever will. Maybe when I am sixty and retired from racing, I will join the fray. But for now I'm content to watch the Miami madness from my balcony and then turn in early so I can get up for a long run on the beach. On the weekends I go to the tennis club and I am happy to say that my game has improved considerably since I was fourteen. I am too competitive to lose, so I have learned to focus on the technique and not just the workout.

One Sunday, I get home from tennis and Kati tells me she wants to go apartment hunting. I am tired and sweaty and that is the last thing in the world I want to do.

"I think I'm ready to stop renting and to buy something," Kati says. "Will you come look with me?"

"Do I have to?"

"You've lived here longer than me. I need your help!"

"Okay, fine, give me a minute." I take a quick shower, change, and grudgingly accompany Kati on an impromptu apartment hunt.

We get to the first place. I tell her, "This one looks good. Take this one."

She rolls her eyes at me. "No, Helio, I don't like it. You have to really help me; don't just say you like everything so we can go home."

Kati likes the next place, but I think it's way too expensive. This is going to take forever! I suggest we make a bet. "Kati, if I win Indy this year, I will buy you an apartment."

She stares at me a moment to see if I am serious. I know it is a big bet for a guy with the nickname Cheapskate, but I figure it is a win-win situation. I hold out my hand and we shake on it.

∫

In order to make all of the CART and IRL races during the 2001 season, we travel almost nonstop. On May 6, we have a CART race in Nazareth, Pennsylvania, and then we fly straight to Indy to qualify. Gil and I change our suits on the plane and as soon as we land we get in a car and head for the speedway for qualifying rounds.

Roger drives us through the speedway on his golf cart and I am once again impressed by the immensity of the place. Roger knows it like the back of his hand. We pass from the garages, through Gasoline Alley, and into the stadium. We walk through the infield and all of the fans and crew members are calling out, "Roger, you're back! Great to have you back!" Team Penske has not entered Indy since 1995—and that year they didn't race because both drivers failed to qualify. This makes the team very anxious about qualifying. There are two qualifying weekends at Indy, but we are able to make it only to the first one, this weekend. We will be going to Japan for another CART race the next weekend. This is our only shot.

At a lot of races, the qualifying is limited to a certain window of time and a certain amount of laps. But at Indy in 2001, there are limitations. Because we are worried about qualifying, we get right down to business. We run so much that Gil and I start to come up with lame excuses so that I can rest for a minute or two. I complain that I need new tear-off pads on my helmet to wick away the sweat. I tell them that first gear needs to be changed, though I only use first gear when I leave the pit lane, so clearly it is not worn out. I just need a moment to break and clear my head.

When it comes to qualifying, I know that I just have to hold on for four laps. Gil goes first and he comes in at fifth place. I go after him, and post at eleventh place.

I'm not happy with it. I keep telling Roger that I have to go back and get a higher position.

"No," he says. "You're fine. As long as you're on the line, that's all that matters."

⌡

We fly to Japan on Monday morning. It is a fourteen-hour flight from Indiana and when we get there I am discombobulated. The race in Japan is on Saturday, so we have a few days to get used to the time difference before we race. We practice for several days and during the qualifying round, I secure the pole position. If only I had done this well last week at Indy!

I start on the pole and run a tight race, finishing in second. As I am in the media center, talking to the reporters, one of our PR representatives pulls me away. "Sorry to interrupt, folks, but we have to go back to America now for the last Indy practice," she says.

We fly back to Indianapolis and arrive on Saturday night. We gain a day because of the time difference. Now I am really disoriented. We go to our hotel to try to sleep. I wake up Sunday morning tired, groggy, and jet-lagged. But this is our last day to practice on the speedway before the race the following Monday. We want to get in as much track time as possible.

When I was leaving Japan, a guy gave me a caffeine pill that he told me would help me avoid the jet lag. So I take one of the pills before heading for the track. It is the first time I have taken anything like this in my life and I am surprised when it actually works. Maybe a bit too well. I am hyper by nature and this stuff makes me go into overdrive. I am talking in fast-forward. I get a speeding ticket on the way from the hotel to the track. I try to explain myself to the officer, but my words are running together. "I'm sorry but I just got back from Japan and I'm jet-lagged and I'm trying to get to the racetrack because I have to practice and I'm a race driver and I took this stuff and . . ." On and on I go. The officer looks at me like I'm a madman and hands me my ticket.

When I arrive at the track, I feel like I am out of my body. I start to drive and am posting 218, 219, 220—pretty fast, but I know I'm taking a lot of unnecessary chances. I stop the car and ask the team, "How is Gil doing?"

"Two hundred," Cindric tells me. "Not good." Gil stops his car. He is moving in slow motion.

"I have to go home," he says to Cindric. "For a few days, I have to go back to Miami and rest. I am in no condition to drive right now."

"Wait! You cannot go home," I say, still talking fast. "We have to practice. If I am practicing, you have to practice."

Gil looks at me, then at Cindric. "I have to go home," he says again.

I look at Cindric. "I can't focus, either."

"Get out of here. Go. You guys are useless," he says jokingly.

We both go home to Miami for four days. We have been traveling for a month straight. We are able to recoup and get our energy back. We return for Carburetion Day, or Carb Day, the Friday before the race. I am back to normal, back to speaking at a normal pace. I am ready to race.

ſ

The day of the 500, I wake up at 6 a.m., anxious to get to the track. "We need to beat the traffic," I tell everyone. It is a cool, overcast morning in Indianapolis. I can feel the butterflies in my stomach as I walk toward the speedway with Gil and Kati. I start to sing my favorite song to calm myself. I only know the first verse and repeat it over and over again. *"Here's a little song I wrote, / You might want to sing it note for note. / Don't worry, be happy."*

"Helio." Gil interrupts me on the twelfth round of "Don't Worry, Be Happy." He holds a finger to his lips. "Shhh. For one minute, just shhh."

"Okay," I say, and I start to whistle instead.

Gil turns to my sister. "Kati, there is something wrong with your brother."

"Yes, I am aware." She yawns. "Helio, it's early. Please."

"Okay, okay," I say. I keep quiet for a moment and then start to hum softly.

I have too much nervous energy to be completely quiet. Gil and Kati give up on it. But then we walk into the racetrack and I finally fall silent. The Indianapolis Motor Speedway is larger than life, large enough to make even me speechless. I pause in reverence each time I enter it. Especially on this day.

We have been practicing on the track all week, but this is the day of the Indy 500. The vibe is different. It is only seven in the morning and already the air hums with excitement. It is my first 500, and I have the confident feeling that every little thing really is going to be all right. I hum my song in my head. There are still butterflies in my stomach. But that is my favorite part of racing. If you can allow for the butterflies and still maintain control, it means you are going to be sharp for the action. I tell myself, as I have at every race before this one, that I will race with a feeling of confident control. Otherwise there is no point in even going to the starting line.

ſ

The cold temperatures cause problems in the race from the beginning. During the first eighteen laps, there are three crashes. I manage to stay in the top ten and on lap 107 the yellow flag comes out, indicating that the field has to slow down and nobody is allowed to pass. At that point I am in second and Gil is in first. But then rain begins to fall on the track and the officials declare a rain delay.

We pull into the pits to wait out the rain. After about twenty minutes the race is restarted. Gil and I hold on to first and second until lap 134, when we are penalized on one of the pit stops because I come out of the pit box into the second lane. It is a necessary move, so that I don't crash with Gil. Still, it is costly. Tony Stewart takes the lead. But in lap 149, Tony pits and I fly out in front. I am in first as it starts to rain even harder than it did the first time, and am holding the lead at lap 155 when the officials declare another rain delay. Indy rules state that if the race is more than halfway finished, a winner can be declared. When I pull into the pits for the delay, I see a little hole of sunshine in the sky and I know the race is not over. My dad is all worked up, though. "We are going to win!" he tells me. "We are going to win!"

"Okay, Dad, calm down," I say. "Just stay cool. We are going to go back. The rain is going to stop."

Fifteen minutes later we start up again. I am in the lead and Robbie Buhl is on my tail. I am having a hard time keeping him behind until he spins out and I can finally relax. For the next forty laps I don't look back. When I cross the finish line, I unbuckle myself to run to the fence. When I get there, I start to climb and I call my teammates to climb with me, too. It is an incredible feeling to hear the stadium of nearly four hundred thousand people cheering for me.

I look around for my family and see they are rushing toward the winner's circle. Dad is beaming from ear to ear. Mom is crying. Kati hugs me and starts to say, "You know . . ."

"I know, I remember. I owe you an apartment."

A track official puts a wreath around me and somebody else hands me a pint of milk. I remember watching this exact scene play out on TV in 1989, when Emerson won his first Indy. And I realize that there are fourteen-year-old kids all over the world watching me right now, fantasizing about being in my position. I realize I am living out a dream.

I know that the Indianapolis 500 is bigger than any other race in North America, but I am not fully aware of how winning it will shift my world. All of a sudden there are banquets in my honor.

The PR team starts receiving phone calls from all of the big magazines: *Maxim, Sports Illustrated, Details.* Fans begin to notice me in airports and shopping malls. People ask for my autograph a lot more and stop me, asking if I will pose for pictures with them. It seems like only yesterday that I was destined for obscurity and headed back to Brazil with my family to figure out how I was going to make a living. Now I am being treated like a rock star. It takes me by surprise at first, but I am all too happy to go along for the ride.

People magazine calls me to be a part of their Sexiest Men Alive issue. "Oh man," I say with a laugh. "Are you serious? Do you have the right number?"

"Yes, we want to feature you as 'Sexiest Race Car Driver.'"

I think, wow, my friends are going to have a field day with this.

A crew comes to my apartment for a photo shoot and the photographer keeps telling me, "Look out on the horizon.

Look out on the horizon." Over the course of an afternoon, I become a model. It is my first taste of anything beyond the racing world, and I love it. My friends and teammates all make fun of this, of course. "Don't worry," I say to them. "You're jealous. I understand. You'll get it next year."

My family thinks it is all very entertaining. To them I am still little Helihno (and always will be). They are not about to let any of my newfound notoriety go to my head. When I get back to Miami everyone wants to throw me a party. At one party I enter the banquet hall and after ten minutes, I realize that I don't know anybody in the room. I stand in the corner, sipping a seltzer water and wondering when I will be able to make my exit.

A woman stands nearby, looking out of place, too. "You look just as bored as I am," I say.

"Well, I don't really know anyone here," she tells me.

"Me neither," I say. I notice that everything about her is striking: her blond hair, her brown eyes, her bright smile.

"Wait, isn't this your party?" she replies.

"Yes, I guess so. But I really don't know anyone else here."

Immediately she backs away. The fact that I am a race car driver seems to repulse her. Now, of course, I am eager to prove that I am a nice, normal guy. We talk for the rest of the night and we begin to casually date. It is the only kind of relationship I am capable of at the moment. I don't yet know how to balance out my personal and professional lives. Racing comes first.

⌠

After the 2002 season, my contract is up with Penske. When I originally signed with the team, I told Roger that my ultimate goal was Formula One. So when I ask him if it is okay to go for a Formula One test before renewing our contract, he tells me to go ahead and give it a shot. I am grateful that he follows through on his word.

I go to France to test with the Toyota Motorsports at the Paul Ricard Circuit. From the start, it is going incredibly well, so well that toward the end of the test, the mechanics are clapping for me. When I stop the car I think I have it locked up. We have a lunch break and during the break, the team manager tells me, "You are doing really well. Much better than we expected for never having driven a Formula One car."

"Thanks," I say. "I know that you have already filled one seat, but what about the second one? What are my chances?"

I am really just trying to make conversation, so I am shocked when he answers, "Actually, we just signed someone this morning."

"What do you mean? When I came here, you told me there was a seat open."

"Yes, but we had been talking to Cristiano da Matta and he signed with us a few hours ago." I feel as though he has just poured a bucket of cold water on me.

"What am I doing here, then?" I ask.

My dad is sitting next to me, and though he doesn't understand English, he somehow understands what has happened.

"Let's get out of here," my father says. I may be upset, but my father is livid.

"Calm down, Dad. You know what? Let's just finish the test." I know it might be the last time I get the chance to drive Formula One. I get back in the car and am very relaxed, since now I know I have nothing to lose. I start to really have fun and don't hold anything back. All right, I think, let's see how fast this thing can go!

I am a man possessed. I am pushing the car to the limit, banging the wheels on the curbs, cornering at top speed. When I stop, the mechanics inform me that I am only a second off the track record. "Let's go out again. I can't break it!" I say.

"We have run out of mileage on the engine," they tell me. "The car is done."

I may have been new to F1, but I was not new to racing. I know the car could go another couple of laps. "Come on, I can do two more laps. Now I understand the track and the car; I just need new tires to push it." They have to call some guy in Germany for permission. Fifteen minutes later they come back and tell me he has cleared it. "Okay, let's go," the engineer says.

I put my helmet on and jump in the car. Everyone is excited and buzzing around. "Let's do it! Come on, man!" they are telling me.

I am amped up. But as soon as I leave the pits, the engine stops altogether. It doesn't sputter or stall; it just plain gives out on me. I get out of the car and tell my father, "You know what? That's it. It's a sign. It's not meant to be. I got an opportunity. I went for it. But Formula One is not in the cards for me."

When I come back to the States, I tell Roger, "I'm staying with you. You treat me fairly. You are loyal. You just can't beat that." For so many years, my dream has been Formula One. I surprise myself at how calmly I am able to let it go.

I decide to spend some of my Indy winnings and so buy my first hot car. A blue Ferrari. Late one night, I am stopped at a traffic light on U.S. Route 1 in Miami. I look to the left at the car stopped beside me. A sleek silver Porsche. Wow, nice wheels. I look up to the driver. A gorgeous, wavy-haired brunette. Wow, nice woman. Our eyes meet and I

COURTESY OF THE AUTHOR

Christmas with Kati at home in Ribeirão Preto.

COURTESY OF THE AUTHOR

Kati and Me in São Paulo, 1975.

COURTESY OF THE AUTHOR

1987—Dad is my promoter.

My first big win!

COURTESY OF THE AUTHOR

The kids of São Paulo.

COURTESY OF THE AUTHOR

My first trophy!

In my first go-kart with Tio Guaraná.

COURTESY OF THE AUTHOR

COURTESY OF THE AUTHOR

COURTESY OF THE AUTHOR

Kati and me in Formula 3 years.

COURTESY OF THE AUTHOR

With Ayrton Senna.

COURTESY OF THE AUTHOR

At the track in Silverstone, England, with Mom and Kati.

COURTESY OF THE AUTHOR

Team Corpal Formula Chevrolet.

COURTESY OF THE AUTHOR

Preparation.

COURTESY OF THE AUTHOR

Ready to race.

COURTESY OF THE AUTHOR

Celebrating after Richmond 2005.

En route to my third Indy.

IMS PHOTO BY JIM HAINES

Spider-Man.

IMS PHOTO BY SHAWN PAYNE

IMS PHOTO BY JIM HAINES

Milk never tasted so good.

Ring number three!

IMS PHOTO BY RON MCQUEENEY

Victory!

CAROL KAELSON / DISNEY ABC TELEVISION GROUP / ABC VIA GETTY IMAGES

COURTESY OF THE AUTHOR

*The Castroneves family
welcoming our newest addition!*

COURTESY OF THE AUTHOR

Mommy and Mikaella.

look away. I am still a little shy and am not sure what to do in this situation.

I look back and she smiles.

Wait. Did she smile?

She revs up the car.

No! Is this a dream?

I rev my engine back.

She spins her tires.

What is going on?

At the next traffic light, our eyes meet again. I rev my engine. She revs back. The light turns green and we race to the next one.

Is this really happening? Racing on Route 1 in Miami? I have to call a friend!

"Dude, you won't believe this. There is a hot chick racing me on the street."

"Ask for her phone number!"

Right. Good point.

At the next light, I roll down my window.

"I know who you are. You drive the red and white car."

Wow. She knows her stuff. I am impressed. "What's your number?" I ask.

"Three-oh-five . . . "

And this is the moment when I understand the value of a Ferrari and an Indy ring.

It's obvious that the newfound money and fame come with a few perks, but I do wonder if I will ever manage to balance racing and a nice, normal girlfriend. Every other week I am in a different city; my days are jam-packed with practices and training and media obligations. It is hard to fit a stable relationship into the equation. An athlete's life really doesn't lend itself to the stable relationship track. It not the normal, healthy kind of relationship that people with nine-to-five jobs have. It is the nature of the beast. Plus, once you start to gain notoriety, you are always wondering if the girl is interested in you for your personality or your persona. I am no moron. I know that a woman who rolls down her window and drag-races me is not attracted to my personality, but right now I'm ready to have some fun.

Later that month, I am sitting in class at traffic school in Miami because of a speeding ticket (Kati was in the car to yell at me that time—but I'm sure I was only going a few miles over the speed limit). We are watching a video and I am surprised to see Al Unser Sr., on the screen. "Why do I wear a seat belt?" he is asking us. "To save my life. They saved my life many times."

I read the caption across the bottom of the screen. "Al Unser: Four-Time Winner of the Indianapolis 500."

The instructor pauses the video and asks if we know who Al Unser is.

"I do," I say. But I never mention that I have won Indy that very year. I think how one day it could be me on that video, with a similar caption next to my name. I am beginning to realize just how big Indy is in America and I take up a new goal—I am going to shoot to win Indy as many times as Al Unser Sr., did.

CHAPTER 8

Chasing History

**Winning in my business
is everything.**
—AL UNSER

C AN HE DO IT? the headline reads. "Nobody has won back-to-back Indys since Al Unser in 1971." My face is printed across the front of the newspaper. I pick it up, grab some breakfast, and go back to my rented Indianapolis apartment.

I thought I would know what to expect when I returned to Indy this year. I knew that the crowds would be there on Carburetion Day, the fans would fill up Gasoline Alley, and excitement would be in the air. But I did not anticipate all the hype that would be surrounding me.

I sit in the apartment watching ESPN Classic. A clip of Al Unser's 1971 victory is shown. He starts in the back of the pack and at one point, he is a full two laps down. The race is filled with ugly crashes and the leader blows out his engine with only ten laps to go. The announcers are talking about the fact that Unser is driving a show car, meaning that it had been retired to be on display for sponsor events. But in the end, Unser wins, against all probability.

I flip the channel to ESPN News and the reporters begin to discuss tomorrow's race. "If defending champion Helio Castroneves manages to take the checkered flag this Sunday, he will join an elite club of drivers as only the fifth man to win back-to-back Five Hundreds. It has not been done since 1971, when Al Unser captured his second Borg-Warner trophy. What are his chances? Statistics suggest . . ." I flip the channel again. I don't want to hear what the statistics suggest. I am racing to win and I want to forget about probabilities or what record might be at stake.

But as the hours pass, I cannot escape hearing about the record. Everywhere I go, somebody mentions it to me. And it is the only thing reporters ask me about in the prerace interviews. It becomes more and more difficult to ignore the prospect of joining that select group of back-to-back Brickyard winners: Wilbur Shaw, Mauri Rose, Bill Vukovich, and Al Unser. When I walk through Gasoline Alley into the stadium a massive crowd starts cheering, "Spider-Man! Spider-Man!" The year before the crowd had been half this size. And the fans were not cheering for me; in fact, they didn't even know who I was. Now I am the center of their attention. A chill goes down my spine. I begin to ask myself what the reporters have been asking all week: Will I be the first driver since Al Unser Sr., to win back-to-back? Can I do it? I start to believe I can.

In 2001, I was a rookie with no exposure and no expectation. Now the expectations are enormous and far beyond my imagination. I am really just thrilled that the fans even know my name (though most still cannot figure out how to pronounce it). They cry out to me: "Julio, hello! Giulo, Ellio!" I don't care what they call me, as long as they are cheering for me.

Indianapolis is a place of tradition. The garage area is called Gasoline Alley though the cars haven't run on gasoline in over forty years. The Friday before race day is called Carburetion Day, because it used to be the last day for teams to adjust their carburetors; however, fuel injection systems replaced carburetors in the late 1940s. And the winner drinks a carton of milk because in 1936, winner Louis Meyer asked for a glass of buttermilk in the winner's circle. In 1993, when Emerson won for the second time, he asked for orange juice instead of milk and it caused an uproar. Indy is not a place to shirk tradition.

Before the race begins, Kati says, "We have to bet something." Betting on something has become the Castroneves tradition.

"Okay, what should it be?"

"A car?"

"These bets seem a little one-sided," I joke.

"It worked last year—it should work this year, too."

"Okay," I say. "Deal." We shake on it and I head to the starting line.

I am in the thirteenth position after a less-than-impressive qualifying round but this year I don't care so much. I remember what Roger told me: "You're in the race. That's all that matters." This time I know what I need to do.

Thirteen is a lucky number, I tell myself. Thirteen means I get to pass twelve guys, and I love passing. From the very beginning of the race, it seems that thirteen may not be so lucky for me today. I am facing so many challenges all at once. My car is not handling well at all. The idle of the engine is too low so I am stalling every time I enter the pits. As I am coming in I have to jump-start the car so I won't lose time. It seems that this year it is just not meant to be. But I'm not about to give up just yet, and luckily neither is my team. I am about to be a lap down and Cindric says, "We have to take a chance here. Do you want to do it?"

"Yes," I say. "Put me out front. I'll take care of the rest."

So, instead of pitting, we gamble that my car will be able to finish on what is left in my fuel tank. An engine can usually go about thirty to thirty-two laps on one tank. We hope to stretch it out to forty. We are counting on luck. On lap 177, when everyone else pits, I take the lead. I know I need at least two or three laps of yellow if I am going to stay there. "You have got to save fuel," Cindric keeps saying, in a very stern voice. "You have got to save fuel." I am running at half throttle, but I have stretched my lead to three and a half seconds. I am staring at the light on my steering wheel, waiting for the yellow to flash. I let some lap-down cars pass me so I can draft behind them and save as much fuel as possible. Lap 190, no yellow light. Lap 195, nothing. Lap 196, Cindric tells me, "Paul Tracy's in third and just passed for second. He's gaining. You gotta go. You gotta go." I see Tracy in my mirrors, coming on strong. I make sure to give him the difficult lane of the track so he cannot pass me. We are going flat out and then on lap 198, as we approach turn three, I am still in the lead, and the light starts to flash—yellow, yellow, yellow. A crash behind us has brought out the caution flags. I heave a sigh of relief. Thank you, God.

Then, in the next second, I see Tracy fly by me.

"What's going on?" I scream into the radio. "It's yellow! He passed me under yellow!"

"Don't worry," Cindric tells me. "You've just got to make sure you cross the line. Go real slow. Just get the car across."

I am barely touching the throttle because I don't want to run out of fuel. Felipe Giaffone passes me, too, and then Sam Hornish, Jr. "What is going on?" I am yelling. Cindric keeps telling me not to worry and to just get the car across. Then I see my number on the top of the pylon and I calm down a bit.

When I cross the finish line, I hear the guys screaming through the radio. "You win! You are the two-time champion!" The first car beside me is Al Unser, Jr., and I see him holding up two fingers. I am in another world. There are four-tenths of a gallon of fuel left on my meter; I am not sure I even have enough fuel to do the victory lap. I just barely make it around; then the car stops dead. There is no more gas. I hop out and run to the fence. My father is there, with my whole team, including Roger. Roger has promised me that if I won a second time he would climb with me, and he is true to his word. As we all jump on the fence, I cannot stop crying and laughing. Can you believe it? everyone asks me. And truly, I cannot believe it. It has not sunk in yet.

Everything that happens in the winner's circle is a blur. I feel them put the wreath around me and Mom and Kati come running through the crowd, crying and shouting. A reporter holds a microphone in front of me and asks, "For the last couple of laps, all we kept hearing was 'make mileage, make mileage.' What was going through your mind?"

"You know what, I don't really know," I say. "I can't even tell you." Everyone is swirling around, flashbulbs are going off, somebody hands me the ceremonial carton of milk to drink. "I have no words," I keep saying to the reporters. I think to myself, Do you believe it? Back-to-back! Is this a dream?

When I get to the press conference I find out that Paul Tracy is protesting the race. All the journalists are asking me what I have to say about the controversy.

"What controversy?" I turn to Roger. "What's going on?"

"They are debating if Tracy passed you under green or yellow."

"No way; it was yellow. I'm sure of it."

"I know. Just keep calm."

Roger doesn't want me to answer any questions about it, but the more they ask, the more aggravated I get. I expected a celebration and instead I'm facing doubt and suspicion. I want to say that I had been staring at the light for the last forty laps. I would have never backed off if I didn't see that yellow flashing.

As Tracy's team protests the decision everyone begins to speculate. Did he pass? Was it yellow? I just keep telling my family, "I know he didn't pass me. I'm sure of it."

Late that night, we are still at the track, waiting until a decision is made. At 11 p.m., outside the Marlboro Hospitality Suite, Roger tells us, "You won. It's been decided."

We celebrate all over again. We hug and cheer, and I climb the fence next to the suite. Then, after a long roller coaster of a day, we go back to the apartment. At midnight we get a call from Roger. "Tracy's team is appealing the decision."

The next morning we don't know what to do. Should we celebrate or not? Roger tells me, "Just wait. There is nothing you can do." A bunch of my friends from Brazil have flown in for the race and we meet them for lunch. I cannot eat anything. I just keep running the race over in my head. "I know I won. I wouldn't have given up Indy so easily. I would have gone until I ran out of fuel."

"Don't worry," my mother tells me. "God knows. You have to believe it will work out."

The banquet is that night and I arrive with my friends and family a few minutes before it starts. Nobody is there yet. We haven't eaten anything since noon and my friends are starving. Each table has a plate of chocolate-covered strawberries in the center and my friends are walking around eating them all.

"Oh my God, this is so stressful," one of my best friends keeps saying as he pops one strawberry after another into his mouth. "When are we going to know? Will we find out tonight?"

It turns out we have to wait five long weeks while the league reviews the tapes. I never question that I am the winner, but I have no control over what everyone else believes. I just have to wait for the results to come forward. On July 3, the league throws out Tracy's appeal and officially declares me "the fifth back-to-back champion in Indy history." I tell Tracy, "If I was in your position, I would have done the same thing. I don't blame you." For me, Indy is about racing against the best and I know the best are going to fight for every win.

153

I learn a lot from that race. I learn it is not always about having the fastest car, or starting in the pole position, or leading the most laps. It is about believing in yourself, not giving up, and having a team that will keep fighting along with you. I learn that a lot of guts and a little bit of luck will get you where you need to go. And I learn to trust myself even when others doubt me.

INDY 2003

*There are two races in Indianapolis,
one for the pole and one for the race itself.*
— RICK MEARS

The wonder of Indy is that each year you go back thinking you know what to expect. But each year it gets more dramatic, the hype is bigger, and the level of expectation is heightened.

"Can he do it again?" the reporters are asking this time. "Nobody has ever won three in a row. Will he be the first?" My face is plastered across the billboards, the programs, and the tickets. Every major magazine calls for an interview. I appear on *David Letterman, Live with Regis and Kelly,* and all of the morning shows. I learn to love being on camera; I just hope that the show hosts will speak slowly enough so that I can understand. When I am on Dave, he tells me that I am "batting a thousand," a term I have never heard before. When they explain it to me, it becomes my new favorite American phrase. I hope that I can keep my average up this year.

I have a great car this year and have been driving really strong the past few weeks. I am feeling very good about my chances. The experience of last year's Indy has shown me that anything is possible. If I could win it twice, surely I can win it a third time.

On Pole Day, May 10, the weather is uncooperative. It is incredibly windy, with gusts over thirty miles per hour. At any other time, we would not have even tested. But this is Indy; there will be no deferring to Mother Nature.

It is the most difficult pole position I have ever seen. The wind is not letting up and everybody is crashing. When Gil goes out the first time, he cannot get the car above 190 and that takes away all our confidence. My team and I are waiting for the winds to die down before we go out to the track. However, later in the day it becomes obvious that it is just not going to happen. Tony Kanaan posts an incredible 231.006, which seems improbable in such bad conditions. Everyone is impressed. Fans wave Brazilian flags in the stands. I look over to Cindric, who just shrugs his shoulders and good-naturedly tells me, "What are you going to do?"

"It's time," I say. "Now or never."

"All right. Let's take a chance." We start practicing and tweaking the car, paying attention to all the small details. With two hours left in the qualifying window, we decide to go for it. The conditions are actually getting worse and the wind gusts are going up to forty-five to fifty miles per hour.

The first lap I go out at 232. I guess the wind and I are in cahoots, because I keep the pace for all four laps and post an average speed of 231.724.

When I come across the line, I see the Brazilian flags waving again. Much of the crowd is on its feet, cheering. I am jumping around, and as usual I cannot contain my excitement.

"Nice job," Roger tells me. Then, true to form, he adds, "Calm down. There are still two hours left."

"Nobody is beating that!"

Rick Mears, four-time Indy champion, comes up to me. "Impressive," he says. When Rick Mears comes up to you and says "impressive," it is a humbling feeling. It is an incredible moment tacked on to another incredible moment.

Now the hype really starts to build. When I see the headline CAN SPIDERMAN THREE-PEAT? the adrenaline starts to pump through my veins. The stars seem to be aligning.

Brazil magazine runs an article about Gil, Tony, and me. The title: "Indy 500: Boys from Brazil Raring to Win."

Tony is starting in the second position behind me, while Gil is in tenth. The article focuses mostly on Tony and me. "Mark your calendars for May 25. . . . It will be a superhero face-off . . ."

Two weeks after Pole Day, all three of us are on the speedway once again, listening to our adopted country's national anthem before the 2003 Indy 500. Gil and I stand next to each other. The start of the race is always an awe-inspiring moment. You practice the whole month and the grandstands are empty and gray, but on the day of the race, the stands are full and colorful. The track takes on a whole different dimension.

We start the race and right away I feel that my car is handling really well. I am confident in my chances. I stay in the lead for most of the race. With about forty laps to go, I am holding the lead and Gil is only a few hundredths of a second behind. I make a risky pass in and I nearly make contact with a lapped car. It could have been a disaster. I start talking to myself. "Don't take risks like that, Helio."

With twenty laps to go, there is another pit stop and I take a five-second lead over Gil. There are no more pit stops. I just have to hold on until the finish line. It sounds very simple, but of course it never is. The same lapped car that I passed in that risky move a few laps back is now going into the same turn with me. I take it easy this time, but I don't anticipate that he will take it easy, too. We slow down so much that I have to put the car in third gear (we run most of the race in sixth gear). My five-second lead has turned into a second-place position. I have lost my momentum. I am trying so hard to make up for it and trying to take any chances to pass, but I cannot find an opening.

I finish in second, three-thousandths of a second behind Gil. I cannot believe it. This is the year I had the fastest car, yet I couldn't win; in the past two years my car was not nearly as good. I am a little disappointed, but I'm also happy because as a team we have placed in first and second. And Gil, my good friend, gets the victory.

Not long after this race, Gil says to me, "I'm thinking of packing it in."

"Why the hell would you want to do that?" I say.

"I want to spend time with my family. I'm getting old," he tells me. "You can't do this forever, you know."

But I don't believe him. I cannot imagine a life without racing.

On Trial

**Forgiveness is an attribute
of the strong.**
—MAHATMA GANDHI

FOUR YEARS AFTER Emerson and I had our final discussion in his office in São Paulo, we meet again. This time we are sitting on opposite sides of a Miami courtroom. *Fittipaldi USA, Inc. v. Helio Castroneves.* And *Helio Castroneves v. Emerson Fittipaldi.* His company is suing me; I am countersuing him. It is a huge, tangled mess.

It has been a tumultuous four years since I last spoke to Emerson. On the racetrack I have done very well. But behind the scenes I have been meeting with my lawyers, trying to figure out a way to avoid this trial. I tried to do everything possible to prevent a fight. My lawyers and I made offers, Roger tried to mediate the situation, but in the end, nothing worked. We have to let a jury decide now.

Emerson's attorney, Mr. Davis, stands at the front of the courtroom, giving his opening statement. He wears a power suit and a bow tie. He is poised and well spoken. "I want to introduce the characters in this drama you're going to watch unfold during this week. Mr. Emerson Fittipaldi and Mr. Castroneves. Let me start with Mr. Fittipaldi. Mr. Fittipaldi for thirty-five years was among the foremost race car drivers in the world. . . ."

Davis continues to speak of Emerson's fame and success. He describes how I idolized Emerson, how Emerson offered to take me under his wing, and how excited I was to sign with him. All of this was true. But then he tells the jury, "Mr. Castroneves was going to drive. Mr. Fittipaldi was going to take care of the rest. And that's what he did, and that is what the evidence will show. He arranged for his medical insurance, his liability insurance, his disability insurance. . . ."

"Wait, a minute here," I whisper to Larry. "He did not 'take care of the rest.' And he did not get me any insurance. I didn't have insurance until Penske."

"I know. Don't worry. I know."

"Can't we object?" I have no understanding of trial proceedings (aside from watching *Judge Judy*), and don't know why Larry is not standing up and screaming, "Objection!"

"We can't object," he tells me. "We have to be patient. Just be calm. We will get our chance to tell the truth."

I want to stand up right then and yell to the jury, "It's not true. That's not true!" Instead I have to sit there and listen to Davis continue.

"So they start the ninety-nine season. Mr. Castroneves is doing better than he had done the year before. He got a two-hundred-thousand-dollar salary the year before. Now he's getting two hundred and fifty thousand dollars; he's getting fifty thousand dollars in expense money; he's getting prize money; he's getting the sponsors that Mr. Fittipaldi gave him. . . ."

"Come on! Is this real?" I say to Larry. "I never saw any of that sponsor money!"

"I know, Helio, I know. Don't worry. Be patient."

But I am not good at being patient. And I am not good when things are out of my control. Every fiber of my being wants to scream, "I was supposed to get that money, but I never did because Emerson didn't pay Hogan my sponsor money!"

I fidget in my seat and bite my tongue.

Davis keeps talking: "Now, Mr. Hogan from time to time would get impatient and he would fire off a letter saying you still owe me the million. . . ."

"Okay, finally one part is true," I tell Larry. "That's the first true thing he's said in a while."

I stay quiet after that. I listen to Davis make his opening statement for two more hours. It feels like an eternity. I want to scream a thousand times, "That's not true!" I am angry and anxious, but mostly I am upset.

The worst part is the feeling of being so alone. Kati cannot be there with me because she is being called as a witness. My parents are in Brazil. All my life, my family has been by my side to offer guidance and support. Now I am facing the most difficult time of my life on my own. Meanwhile, Emerson's entire family is in the courtroom. I had been friends with all of them. I understand that they are his family and that they are going to take his side, but it's hard for me to know that they are looking at me as if I'm a cheat and a bad person.

After Davis finishes, Larry stands up to give his opening statement. As he walks to the front of the courtroom, he trips over his cowboy boots. Oh boy, I think. I hold my head in my hands. Now I realize how serious the trial is and I pray that Larry will be able to set the record straight.

Kati comes to my apartment that night, but I am not allowed to discuss the trial with her. All I can say is, "I think I'm going to lose. He has this high-powered attorney. You should hear what he says. None of it true."

My mother calls and comforts me with the same words she always has: *"Deus sabe. Você sabe. A verdade vai prevalecer."* God knows and you know. The truth will prevail.

The next three days pass at an agonizingly slow pace. As each witness takes the stand, I go off on a roller coaster of emotions.

Mr. Goodstadt, Emerson's business partner, is one of the first to testify. As he speaks, it takes everything in me to stay quiet. During the cross-examination, Larry asks him about the contract extension I signed with Emerson in 1998.

Goodstadt answers: "Helio Castroneves was so happy and so excited to get that ride for the next year that he wanted that contract extended, and he said, 'Don't tell my family about it. Let's keep this a secret.'"

"Well, why would he do that?" Larry asks.

"Helio told me all the time that his family was a pain and he didn't want them at the races." I cannot believe my ears. It is the most fictitious statement yet. Blood starts to rush to my head. My family is the reason I am racing at all. They are my support system from the very beginning. To suggest that I would not want them to come to my races is absurd.

It is an infuriating feeling to hear lies spoken about me, as I sit not twenty feet away, forced to stay silent. I bite down on my tongue and repeat my mother's words to myself: "God knows and you know. The truth will come out."

The witnesses for my side begin to testify and I calm down a bit as each of them begins to set the record straight. Roger gives a deposition stating that Emerson had nothing to do with arranging my deal with Penske. Then Alan appears and explains my contracts and my finances. Most of what he is saying is news to me, and honestly, I'm not sure I understand most of the contract and tax information he is talking about. He is speaking in legal terms, which I wouldn't understand even if he were speaking in Portuguese, never mind English.

It is hardest for me to watch Kati up on the stand. I am a mess inside, but she stays calm and composed as she explains things: "I moved from my home to São Paolo to help Mr. Fittipaldi do what he was paid to do, but could not do. And he told me that 'it wasn't as easy as I thought it was going to be.' I got the Consul sponsorship. I told everybody about it. I told Mr. Fittipaldi about it. He was happy."

"Did you take the commission on that Consul sponsorship?"

"No. Mr. Fittipaldi did," Kati explains. "Just like I'd been doing for twelve years, I supported my brother. I moved to Miami the next year to continue to do that. I went to all the races where everything happens, all the deals are made, where you take care of the driver's business."

"But you still paid Mr. Fittipaldi?"

"Of course, of course, I paid what we owed to Fittipaldi USA in ninety-eight and ninety-nine. We keep our promises."

The reality of Kati's situation strikes me. She moved to Miami for me. She worked for free. And then, on top of all of that, I was sending Emerson the checks for the job she was doing herself.

Kati and I make eye contact and she flashes me a broad smile, as if to say, "Don't worry. It's going to be fine."

I then make the mistake of looking over at Emerson, who is glaring at me with a look that seems to say, "Screw you."

My stomach is in knots as Larry walks up to give the closing statement. He is cool, calm, and collected—a stark difference from the first day of the trial. He speaks eloquently about my life, my racing career, and my family.

"We have three undisputed truths here," he says. "One: All Mr. Castroneves wants to do is drive. And he's very, very good at it. Two: He's not really good with contracts. And three: He is a very lucky man, because as he worked his way up the ladder of racing, he did not have to do it alone. He had the support of his family."

I bow my head.

"The evidence shows clearly that Mr. Fittipaldi made misrepresentations from the get-go. 'I've got sponsors. I'll take care of you. No problem. Just drive.' Helio Castroneves kept his promise. 'I'll pay you twenty dollars out of every one hundred.'"

It is the hundredth time the story has been told and it doesn't get any easier to listen to. I kept my promises—of that I'm sure. But it is painful to hear, time and time again, how I have been misled and duped by Emerson. The truth of the whole case is hard to bear. This was a guy I idolized. I imagined that signing with him was going to make all of my problems go away. It would be like when I was on Team Corpal; he would coach me and give me advice on how to get better. I would just have to worry about driving; the sponsorships and the business side would be taken care of for me. And we would have fun. How wrong I had been.

As the jury deliberates I ponder all this. How did it come to this point? That contract I signed with him, which I thought would make all of my problems disappear, became the root of this incredible dilemma.

When the jury foreman stands up to read the verdict, I am extremely tense. Kati and I cannot understand what he is saying. Because there are so many claims, there are a lot of different results. But I understand the most important result very well. "The jury rules that Helio Castroneves did not breach the contract with Fittipaldi USA." I let out a huge sigh of relief. I have gone an entire week without eating or sleeping, just waiting to hear those words. I can breathe again. All I can think is that I never want to go through anything like this again. I don't wish this upon anyone.

However, I soon discover that the fight is not over. This is a nightmare that will not go away. Emerson's lawyers appeal the decision to the Florida Supreme Court. I am worried that this will result in another lengthy battle, but instead the

164

court quickly rules that not only did I not breach the contract, but Emerson has to pay my attorney's fees.

I am, once again, immensely relieved. Yet I don't feel that I have won anything. I only feel that the truth has been revealed, as my mother said it would.

To put the memory of the trial behind me, I decide I need a fresh start and will move out of the apartment I have been in since 1997. I start to look for a house, someplace where my family can gather for the holidays and during the off-season. I find a home in Coral Gables, Florida, and finally make my first major purchase. From here on out, I think, it will be smooth sailing.

I only wish. Six months later, the government sends out one hundred and fifty subpoenas to anybody whom I have dealt with in the past five years. I only learn of it because a car dealer I had once bought a car from calls, saying, "I just got a subpoena asking for any records involving Helio Castroneves."

Then Citibank terminates the company account for Castroneves Racing without explaining why.

"What is that all about?" I ask Alan.

"I'm not sure. But it is curious that this should come so soon after the civil trial."

"Should I be worried?"

"No, not yet."

"Okay then." I forget about it and turn back to racing.

Juan Pablo Montoya and I have stayed friends since we first met at the 1990 World Cup in Italy. He invites me to his charity go-karting race in Cartagena, and I am excited because I have never seen Cartagena and love getting back in go-karts. They make me feel like a kid again.

On my flight from Miami to Cartagena, I notice a beautiful Colombian woman boarding the plane. She has long dark hair, big dark brown eyes, and perfectly pouty lips. She is wearing green army pants and a white tank top, which show off her body in a perfectly understated way. I once read a statistic that one in ten people make a love connection at the airport and I am certain that she is mine. I see her again at the baggage claim. I am trying to think of a good opening line to approach her with, but my friend starts talking to her first. I hear him say, "We are professional window washers." What? That is not quite the opener I was going to use.

She laughs as she grabs her bag. "Ah well. Good luck with your windows." And she waves good-bye.

"Very smooth," I say. "Window washers? What were you thinking?"

"I was being funny. It was funny!"

"Yes, clearly it worked," I say as we watch her walk away.

The event lasts a week and each night there is a dinner, followed by a party. At one of the parties, I bump into the woman again. "Nice to see you again," I say.

"Ah, you are the window washer!"

I laugh. It is much funnier when she says it. I reach out my hand. "My name's Helio."

"I'm Adriana."

We hit it off right away and spend the whole night talking and laughing. She is not only beautiful, but also funny and full of confidence. For the rest of the week we keep crossing paths and whenever we do, we get along as if we have known each other forever. I ask her if she wants to go out on a proper date when we get back to Miami. "I would love to, but I don't live in Miami. I live in Atlanta."

"No problem. I will fly to Atlanta for dinner and a movie with you."

Two weeks later, we have our first dinner-and-a-movie date in Atlanta. It is a perfect first date—there are no awkward silences or uncomfortable moments. We plan another date for two weeks later. Halfway through dinner on the second date, Adriana says, "Listen, I think we should slow down."

Slow down? We have just started! What does she mean "slow down"? The only way I know how to approach a relationship is full throttle. I assume this means she is no longer interested in me. I head back to Miami, wondering where I went wrong.

I head to the track and start running laps—it is the only thing that will help me clear my head. The track is the only place where things always make sense, where I have control, where I know what to do and what to expect, even if the rest of my life isn't running so smoothly.

This same afternoon, my assistant's husband calls her as she is driving home. "Fernanda," he says, "what did you do? There are two policemen at the door. They are asking for you."

When she gets home, the policemen greet her with a subpoena made out to Castroneves Racing. She calls me right away. She is shaken and it takes me a moment to realize what she is saying. I immediately call my lawyer to ask him what we should do. "Shut down the office until I figure out what is going on," he tells Kati and me. It turns out that the government has issued this subpoena because the IRS has not uncovered anything from the 150 subpoenas they sent out earlier in the year. So now they want to look through the company records. Weeks later, IRS agents begin to come to the office and sift through the filing cabinets and computers. Kati keeps me shielded from a lot of what is happening. "You focus on racing. I'll let you know if there is anything you need to know."

"All right," I say, and I turn my energy toward the track. The four-year trial with Emerson has taught me to compartmentalize. There is no way for me to drive successfully if I am always worrying about the business side of things, especially legal issues. I force myself to concentrate on driving and deal with any legal issues as they come along.

The 2006 season starts on May 26 in Homestead-Miami Speedway. During the final minutes of the final practice, a rookie driver, Paul Dana, is fatally injured in a two-car crash. The mood on the track is somber as we are all faced with the reality of our sport—it only takes a split second, one minor mistake. We all strive to put it out of our heads so that we can focus on driving.

Two years ago, I lost this race to Sam Hornish, Jr., in a bitterly close finish. I had led for most of the race, but in the final laps, Hornish took the inside lane and edged out the win.

The race begins much as it did in 2004—I am leading throughout, but this time I am determined not to give up the inside. In the final twelve laps, Dan Wheldon catches up and we are running side by side. There is barely a hair-breadth between his tires and mine. Coming into the final turn, we are still neck and neck. In the homestretch, Wheldon edges me out by .0147 of a second, the ninth-closest finish in IndyCar history. It is an emotional beginning to the season—one where I am reminded of the importance of hundredths of seconds.

I win the next two races—the Streets of St. Petersburg in Florida and the Indy Japan 300 in Motegi, Japan. I have a comfortable forty-two-point lead in the championship standings.

When I get back from Japan, there are IRS agents rifling through the papers in my office. I become anxious.

Almost immediately Adriana and I start dating again. When so much of my life is in turmoil, I am happy to have something so comfortable and secure. Each time the IRS agents come into the office, I get nervous. Why won't this problem go away? What did I do to deserve this? My lawyers are convinced that the issue traces back to the civil case.

I know that it is useless to dwell on a situation I cannot control. Instead, I want to focus on the positive.

I have a commanding lead in the championship standings and the Indianapolis 500 is in three weeks. I remind myself to compartmentalize and maintain my concentration. I have won Indy twice, but the IRL title has always remained just out of reach. I have finished in second, third, fourth, coming close only to have it slip away in the final races. Now that I have a commanding lead so early on, I am hopeful that this is the year I capture the elusive trophy.

Before I head to Indy, I run into an ex-girlfriend, Aliette, at a restaurant in Miami. We had dated on and off for six years and had not seen each other in months. We start talking and I wonder why we ever broke up. I ask her out to dinner the next night and we pick up right where we left off. When so much of my life is in turmoil, I am happy to be in a comfortable and secure relationship.

The rest of the season, half of my life is in order and the other half is up in the air. My personal life is on track, and racing-wise I am doing very well (aside from crashing at Indy and not being able to finish). By the end of the season, I am still in contention to win the championship, but the points race has tightened considerably. I lead by one point; my teammate Sam Hornish is right behind. Dan Wheldon and Scott Dixon are both in the fight, nineteen and twenty-four points back, respectively. It comes down to the last race in Chicago—if I win the race, I win the IRL title.

I battle for the lead the entire race. I have a clear shot at victory when inexplicably, Tony starts to block me. Every time I try to make a move, he sways his car so that I can't pass. Tony is a lap down—he has nothing to gain from blocking me. I don't understand what's happening. It is the final stretch of the race and still he will not let me pass and the officials have not called it. I finish in fourth and lose the title by two points. I am too angry and too dumbfounded to speak. I have to walk away from the track and from Tony. I am afraid what I will say at the moment, but I know that it won't be pretty. It is a horrible end to the season and will cause a rift in our lifelong friendship.

I go back home and find that the IRS investigation has become more intense. "Kati," I ask, "should I be worried? What is going on?"

"I will let you know when you should worry," she tells me.

With so much of my professional life up in the air, I feel like I am ready to settle down in my personal life. For the first time I am in a comfortable relationship and I want to get married and have kids. I propose to Aliette in November 2006 and we begin to plan a wedding for the following year.

Shortly after Aliette and I get engaged, Kati casually says, "You have to come with me to meet with the lawyers. It's about the tax case."

"Okay," I say. "Let me know when." I try to stay calm, but I know this means that the IRS situation must be getting serious. This means I should start to worry.

I head to the track to practice and clear my head. I tell myself not to get worked up just yet. I am going to deal with the situation the only way I know how. Lap by lap. Turn by turn.

CHAPTER 10

Quickstepping

**There is a bit of insanity in dancing
that does everybody a
great deal of good.**
—EDWIN DENBY

I T IS INDY in 2007 and the Olympic speed skater Apolo Anton Ohno has come to see the race. He won the gold medal the year before. He has also just finished season four of *Dancing with the Stars*. I have not watched the show much, though I did tune in a few times when boxer Evander Holyfield was on, just because I wanted to see how a guy like that was going to dance. And I saw a clip of Apolo on CNN dancing the paso doble—I remember it being a pretty impressive, macho kind of dance. All of the news shows were talking about him and I thought, Huh, I wonder if I could do that.

Apolo comes to our garage at the speedway. I am a huge sports fan, so I am always excited to meet athletes from every sport, but this is not just any athlete—this is a gold medalist!

"Hey, man," I say. "I'm a big fan! Congrats on your gold medal. And I saw that you won *Dancing with the Stars*!"

We start talking. I have known him casually before, but this is the first time we have a long conversation. Instead of discussing racing or skating, we discuss ballroom dancing.

"I thought I was well-known after I won the gold medal," he tells me, "but compared to winning *Dancing with the Stars*, the gold medal was nothing."

"No! I don't believe you."

"I swear. You know what? *You* should do it! You would be perfect for it."

"I don't know, man. Ballroom dancing?"

"I'm telling you, it was one of the best experiences of my life. It more fun than you could imagine. The people are all great. It's intense, though. You practice ten hours a day."

"Ten hours?"

"Yeah, in the end it's ten, twelve hours a day."

"That's insane." I think, This is an Olympic athlete. He sure went overboard. He is used to ten-hour training days, so it is normal for him. I never train for more than two hours a day—no way could it be ten or twelve hours!

"So, do you want to do it? I can call the casting director."

"I'm racing in two hours, Apolo. I don't know."

"You should do it. I'm going give them a call. I'll just tell them that you might be interested."

"Oh, sure. Tell her." I head toward the track and switch into racing mode. I am starting in the pole position and hope this will be the year when I get my third Indy win.

I am surprised when I find out that Apolo really does call the casting director, Deena. She watches the prerace video. This year, the video plays up the differences between my teammate Sam Hornish, Jr., and me. They have footage of Sam in a pickup truck, while I am in a Lamborghini. He is in the fields in Ohio, while I am on the beach in Miami. He is quiet and introverted, while I am talkative and extroverted. Deena calls me soon afterward and asks if I would consider being on the show. The *Dancing with the Stars* producers like the video and they think my personality is right for the show. Am I interested? "Sure," I tell her. Why not?

I tell Kati and Aliette about the conversation and they tell me at the same time, "You can't dance!"

"You're crazy! I can too."

It is the middle of the season and I am focused on racing, and every few weeks I have to go into my lawyers' office to discuss the IRS tax case. Plus, Aliette and I are not getting along too well. There is so much going on in my mind and I completely forget about the *Dancing with the Stars* conversation. A month and a half later, I get another call from Deena. "So, do you want to do it?"

"Just like that? I don't have to test or anything?"

"No, just come and meet with us in L.A. and you're in."

"I have to talk to my team, my sponsors, my lawyers. I have to make sure it's okay with everyone." As I say it, I realize how many people I have to pass through before making any decision. There is no way they are all going to be okay with it.

"Okay, let me know as soon as you find out."

Kati and I talk to my team first, and then my sponsors. Much to my surprise, they are all for it. The whole league is really excited, because it will be a chance to introduce Indy to a whole new audience. My lawyers are a little hesitant, but then lawyers are a little hesitant about everything (I speak from a lot of experience here).

For the past few months, Kati and I have been meeting with our lawyers about the IRS issue. I really don't believe anything will come of the investigation. I'm not in denial; I'm just being optimistic. During the meetings, I usually stay quiet and try to understand what is going on. The lawyers and Kati discuss my finances and business dealings. Sometimes they ask about racing; when they do, I come alive. These are questions I can answer with certainty. I light up and start to tell them stories about everything from go-karts to Indy. I will do anything to keep the conversation away from tax issues. Who wants to talk about taxes when you can talk about racing? Or soccer? Anything has to be more interesting than going over "constructive receipts" for the tenth time.

At a meeting in early August, I announce, "So, I've been asked to go on *Dancing with the Stars*."

Silence.

Then Mark Seiden speaks up, both as a friend and attorney. "I'm not sure it's a good idea. It will draw too much attention to you. That's not what you need right now."

Kati's lawyer, Howard, disagrees. "No, I think he should do it. It will show his personality."

It erupts into a heated discussion as all of the lawyers discuss the pros and cons of me going on a reality show. I feel like I am eleven years old again and watching my parents argue over whether I should be able to go to the go-kart track.

"But if he gains more notoriety, it might push the IRS to bring the case to trial."

"But if the case does go to trial, it would only help if his personality was out there."

"What do you mean 'if the case goes to trial'?" I ask. "I thought it wasn't going to trial?"

"There is always the chance. It's not likely, but it may happen."

"Still, it's a gamble to bring any attention to yourself when the IRS is already watching you." David shakes his head.

"Okay, then let's gamble," I say.

Amazingly, everyone is on board—from my lawyers to my pit crew. I call Deena and tell her, "Okay, I'm in."

I don't know what I'm getting myself into, but I'm excited about the new challenge. My whole life has been about driving; this is a very big step outside my comfort zone. I throw up my hands and decide to go along for the ride.

I have a race in Sonoma in late August and afterward, Kati and I fly to Los Angeles with my publicist, Susan. We meet with Deena and the producers for lunch and to go over the contracts. We all like each other from the start. They tell me a bit more about the show. They ask me about my career. We trade stories back and forth—it's a fun meeting and a welcome relief from all the legal meetings I have had to sit through. I happily sign all the paperwork and am ready to leave when they ask me, "Do you want to meet your partner?"

"I thought I was just coming for lunch."

"No, no. She is here. She can meet you now if you want."

"Well, then, sure, I want to meet her."

They introduce me to Julianne Hough and I recognize her as Apolo's partner from last season. Half of me is thinking, Yes, I have the champion. The other half is thinking, Shit, I have the champion. Now I have a lot of pressure.

Julianne and I connect immediately. We have the same kind of personality—cheerful, talkative, a bit hyper. And she is gorgeous. This could be trouble! However, there is a bit of a communication barrier. She is having trouble understanding what I say because of my accent, and I am having trouble understanding what she says because she talks so fast! The producers tell us, "Why don't you try a dance?"

"What? Are you kidding?" I say.

"No, no. That's a good idea," Julianne says. She stands in front of me and tells me, "Okay, grab my hips and put your legs between my legs."

"Uh, wait a minute. I'm not comf—"

"Don't think about it. Just relax."

Right . . .

Within the first few steps I am dancing. I cannot believe it! "Oh, man," I say. "I can do this! I'm dancing! I'm ready!"

"When do you want to start practicing?" Julianne asks.

"Oh, wait. We have to hold on a little bit. I still have two more races. I can't practice much until the season is over."

"Okay, when's that?"

"The last race is in Chicago in two weeks."

The head producer says, "We should have footage of that. Julianne should go to the race!" So we agree she'll come to Chicago and afterward we'll go to Miami and start practicing.

"I'll send you some tapes to look over," Julianne tells me before we say our good-byes.

"Helio," Deena asks me as I am walking out, "I forgot to ask you. Would you mind wearing sequins?"

"Of course, yes. No problem." I nod my head and smile, as I always do when I don't understand the English.

When we are in the car, Kati asks me, "Do you know what sequins are?"

"No, what?"

"Remember the sparkly outfits I used to wear in ballet?"

"Oh no! Those are sequins?"

"Yup."

"I don't have to wear them, do I?"

"Yes! You just told them you would!"

As if I'm not already in over my head with the dancing part, now I have to do it while wearing sequins?

When Julianne sends a DVD with dancing instructions, I rush over to Kati's house, excited for the opportunity to take my mind off other things. "We have to start practicing!" I tell her.

"We should watch the old episodes first," Kati tells me. "That way we know what the show is all about." In addition to the dance instructional, Julianne has sent a set of DVDs of all the episodes from last season. Kati, her husband, Eduardo, and I sink into their couch and watch all the episodes back to back—it is hours upon hours of dancing. Kati is loving it. I am getting a bit nervous as I watch each dancer get better and better. Eduardo looks like he is about to fall asleep.

Then we put in the DVD. Kati is following along with Julianne's instructions, perfectly imitating everything that Julianne does. I am falling over my own two feet. "I can't get it. Show me again," I say to Kati. She rewinds and I try again. "This is impossible," I say. "My feet won't move like that."

Eduardo stands up from the couch. "Let me try." Right away, he starts to quickstep along with Kati.

Now my competitive side kicks in. "Well, if you can do it, I can do it! Rewind it again, Kati!"

We start it over again. Kati and Edu catch on immediately. I am trying like mad to keep up. As soon as I understand what my feet are supposed to do (or when I get frustrated because I don't understand at all), I say, "Okay, next one." We go through each dance that way. We are three loons quickstepping, fox-trotting, and waltzing our way across the family room for hours. If anyone looks in the windows, I am sure they will have us committed. I am awful, but I am having a lot of fun at it. "My God, I better not be the first one off. That's all I ask. I don't want to be the first one kicked off."

That night, I go out to dinner with a few of my racing buddies—Oswaldo and Gil. I wait until halfway through the meal to tell them. "Guess what." I pause for dramatic effect. "I'm going to be on *Dancing with the Stars*."

"What? What's that?" Gil asks. He never watches TV, so he has no idea what I am talking about.

"It's a dance competition reality show," Oswaldo explains. "My daughters watch it."

"But you can't even dance!" Gil tells me.

"I can so dance!" I get up in the middle of the restaurant and start to show them my newly acquired waltz moves.

"Man, you're crazy. Sit down. We're in a fancy restaurant!"

"You know over twenty million people watch that show?" Oswaldo says.

Gil laughs. "Oh man, you are going to make a fool of yourself! In front of twenty million people!"

"You'll see," I say. "I'm going to surprise you! I will not be eliminated first. I can promise that!"

I think I am telling it to myself more than to anyone else.

After my final race, Julianne comes to Miami. I have less than two weeks to learn the fox-trot and I am prepared to work on it all day, every day. It is a difficult dance because there is so much technique involved. I approach it the same way I approach racing—she is my coach; I am the student. I keep a notebook, just as I do during the racing season. I write down the steps and reminders: *Right, left, right. Left, right, left. Turn. Go straight.*

The first few days, we are getting to know each other. We are having fun, joking with each other, and flirting a bit. We also practice for three or four hours. When I get home, I take out my notebook and practice for three more hours in my bedroom. I want to make her proud, just like with every coach I have had in the past. I want to show her that I am working hard. On the fourth or fifth day, I am getting anxious. "I think we need to practice longer," I tell her. "Apolo told me he practiced ten hours a day."

"Don't worry; you're fine. Toward the end, we practice ten hours a day. But if we do that now you'll burn out."

"But the other guys have been practicing for weeks. I can't be kicked off first!" That is obviously my main concern.

"Trust me; you'll be fine. If we practice any longer, you'll get frustrated and we will start to fight. It won't be good."

I'm not so sure. The next day I put up the same fight.

"One more hour," I tell Julianne when she says we should stop. "At least one more hour."

"Helio, it's like a race. You can't go full throttle at the beginning. You have to save fuel, develop a strategy, and then at the end we'll have enough left to go flat out."

Clearly she has been talking to Kati a lot. Whenever someone has trouble getting through to me, Kati tells them to put it in racing terms. It always works and this time is no different. I completely understand Julianne's reasoning now.

After two weeks of practice, I am sore all over. I thought I was in shape before, but this is a whole new ball game. I am using muscles I didn't even know I had.

It turns out that *Dancing with the Stars* has come my way at the perfect time. I need something to distract me from my personal problems. My life is in overdrive. I'm in the hunt for the 2007 championship, Aliette and I are having even more issues in our relationship, the IRS investigation is starting to pick up again, and now *Dancing with the Stars*?

My commitment to my professional life has become bigger than my commitment to my personal life. Aliette becomes frustrated that I am spending so much time with Julianne. She begins to not trust me. Nothing I say will ease her mind. It both frustrates and angers me. I have done nothing wrong! Right before *Dancing with the Stars* begins, we decide to call off the wedding. It is a very difficult decision, but certainly the right one for everyone.

∫

Two days before the first show, Julianne and I fly out to Los Angeles. We have rehearsals that Sunday and the girls go first—Jennie Garth, Marie Osmond, Jane Seymour, Sabrina Bryan, Mel B. They are all so good! I start to freak out. "Don't watch the guys," Julianne tells me. "If you think they are better than you, you'll get nervous and make mistakes. And if you think you are better than them, you'll get cocky and then you'll make mistakes." The following day, I keep my head bowed as the guys take the floor—Floyd Mayweather, Mark Cuban, Wayne Newton, and Cameron Mathison.

After rehearsal, I plan to meet for a late dinner at the Ivy with Jennie Garth and her husband. Jennie is running a little late and while Kati and I are waiting for her, the maître d' approaches our table. "I'm sorry; it is too late. We are closing."

"We're waiting for a friend," I tell him. "She'll be here any minute."

"I'm sorry but the kitchen has been closed."

At that moment, Jennie comes running in. "I'm so sorry! I got held up!"

As soon as the maître d' sees her, he does a 180. "Nice to see you, Ms. Garth! Sit down. Can I get you anything to drink?"

The kitchen opens back up and the waiters spring into action. The whole scene is fascinating to me. Kati laughs. "So much for you being a 'star.'"

I wake up the next morning with a pit in my stomach. I am ten times more restless than I have ever been before a big race. At rehearsal that day, the butterflies really start to flutter.

Driving a car at two hundred and fifty miles per hour is dangerous, but dancing in front of twenty million people? Now, *that* scares me. I know what to do when I step into my car. When I step into a ballroom, on the other hand, I'm a rookie. But in many ways, racing has prepared me well for the ballroom. I know how to put the nerves aside, focus on the details, and forget the fear. On the track, I never think about crashing, because I will inevitably crash. I use the same mentality on the dance floor. I remind myself not to think about making a misstep; just keep the pace.

When they announce, "Dancing the fox-trot, Helio Castroneves and his partner, Julianne Hough," the adrenaline starts to pump. As soon as I hear the first note of the song, it is like the flag has been dropped. My competitive drive goes into full force. I am hitting every step. When I finish, the crowd is standing and cheering. I surprise myself and I think I surprise the judges, too. The first thing they say is, "You're a natural." They give us 8, 9, 8. It is the highest score of all the men and the second-highest score of the night. I am pumped. All of those times I told my friends and family, "Just watch, I'm going to win this thing," I was joking around. After I saw those scores and heard the judges' compliments, I gain confidence and think maybe I really can do it.

After that first dance, I start to get more texts than when I won an Indy.

"Okay," I say, "now this is serious. I can't be flying back and forth between Miami and L.A. every week. I have to stay here and really dedicate myself." I move into a hotel near the ABC lot and take my mind off everything else. My broken engagement, racing, the investigation—all of it falls by the wayside. I become obsessed.

♪

Week two is the mambo and it is completely different from the fox-trot. The fox-trot movements are longer and smoother. The mambo is quick and the steps are much more intricate. Julianne keeps telling me, "The expectations are high this week because we scored high last week. We have to push it to the limit." So much for taking it easy! But I only have four days to learn all the steps and I am not getting it nearly as easy as I did the fox-trot.

"I think the choreography is too hard," I tell her. "I can't get it."

"No, you can do it. I'm sure you can. If it takes me ten seconds to learn, I know you can do it. If it takes me a minute to learn, I know it's too hard for you."

"Okay, you're the boss," I say. By the end of the second day, I am starting to pick it up.

When it comes to the night of the show, I have the mambo down pat. The judges give us 9, 9, 9. It is just like a race. We started out strong; then we took the lead, and now we have to keep the pace. I get a message from Apolo: "That was great! Keep up the good work." I am showing all of my friends. "Can you believe this! I got a text from a gold medalist! What is going to be next?"

But week three is the jive and things start to fall apart.

Julianne is giving me so many instructions at once. "Head up, chest out, stay on the beat!"

When I speak to Kati, I tell her, "It's getting a little intense. Julianne is yelling so many things at me. I'm not getting it."

"You have to understand, Helio. It is so easy for her. She was practically born doing these moves. Just be patient and listen to her. She knows what she's doing."

I go back to practice the next day and no matter how much she pushes me, I try to keep up. I can see that her patience is wearing thin. I know that she has a lot going on in her life and I can tell she's exhausted. She has so much to do for the show each week. It is not just about teaching me to dance. She is also in charge of choosing the song, planning the choreography, picking out the outfits. Then she has dances to perform in the middle of the show. On top of that, she broke up with her boyfriend and she is signing her first deal with a record company. I know that she is stressed-out and I remind myself to be patient and focus on dancing.

Week five is the rumba. It is the hardest dance yet. I have to learn to move slowly. The technique has to be perfect because all the mistakes will be very clearly seen. Each step really matters. I learn the dances by flowing with the music instead of counting. When she moves, I move along with her. However, I cannot find the rhythm of the rumba. Plus, I am supposed to look sexy while I doing the steps. "Find a character," Julianne keeps telling me. "Stop smiling! You have to be sexy! No smiling! Shoulders back."

"Wait a minute—now I have to be a dancer and an actor?"

Julianne is getting frustrated with me and starts to point her finger in my face. Okay, I think, this is going a little too far. I have to say something. I know enough about the rumba to know that chemistry matters; it will be the worst dance to have friction between us. That night I call Apolo and ask him for advice.

"Listen, man, I don't know if it's me, but did you and Julianne start to have a little bit of tension?"

"Yeah, it happens. For me it happened in week eight or nine, though, more toward the end. I'm surprised it happened this early."

"What did you do?"

"I had one of the producers talk to her and tell her to ease up a bit. After that it got much better."

I'm happy to know that it's not just me. I decide that instead of having a producer talk to Julianne, I'll wait for an opening during practice and talk to her myself.

The next day is the final day of rehearsals before the show. I am still missing the same step I've been missing all week and Julianne is slapping me on the shoulder each time. "Shoulders back! Shoulders back!"

"Okay, let's have a break," I say.

"No, no, no. You started with the left and you were supposed to go right. Let's go back to the first step."

"I know what I did wrong on the first step, but it's this last step I can't get."

"Fine. Let's have a break. You have to relax. You are thinking too much."

I mumble under my breath, "Yes, I'm thinking how I'm going to get out of here."

"What did you say?"

"I said I'm thinking of how I can get out of here. I've had enough. You are driving me crazy."

"You can't talk to me like that. You don't know me well enough."

"You are right. But I can't relax when all you are telling me is 'this is wrong,' 'that is wrong,' 'stop smiling!' All you tell me are the bad things. What am I doing right?"

"Apolo liked when I did that."

"I'm not him. I learn in a different way. I need something positive to go off of. I am here to have fun. This is not fun for me."

I can see that her eyes are starting to water and I think maybe I'm being too rough. I calm my voice and explain: "I'm just telling you, sometimes you have to compromise. I am not a professional dancer. I am trying my best. If I put you in a race car, you wouldn't be able to go two hundred and twenty miles an hour. How would you feel if I was screaming at you, 'What is wrong with you? Why are you going so slow?'"

She doesn't say anything.

"Listen," I tell her. "For me this is more than a competition. We have become friends and that's why I'm talking to you about this. I could just let it go, but as friends I think it's best to talk this through."

"I'm sorry. That is how I learned to dance. I didn't know you weren't having fun."

"What? I didn't hear that? Did you say, 'I'm sorry'?"

We start laughing, but the tension is still there. When we run through the dance in rehearsals the next day, we don't have the same chemistry as we did in the past and I start to really worry.

Of course, this is the dance that Roger has come to see. He will not sit in the front row, because he is so nervous. Kathy, his wife, and her friend sit in the front and Roger sits behind with Kati. He is telling her, "I can't believe I'm nervous. Why am I nervous?"

When the music starts, I am stiff from the first step. Throughout the entire dance, I know that we are off. When it ends, we stand in front of the judges and I prepare myself. Of course we get our lowest scores yet: 8, 7, 8. The audience starts to boo the judges, but I know they are right. Over it all, I hear Roger booing the judges loudest of anyone. Afterward Roger tells me, "Don't worry. This is just a bad pit stop. It's a long race."

"You know what you need?" Kathy says. "You need a change. You should move to the hotel where we are, closer to the beach. You'll be much more relaxed." She knows my personality so well. Whenever I get overwhelmed, I need to reset everything.

So I pack up all of my things and move to Shutters in Santa Monica. I get a new rental car and when I come back to practice the next morning, I say to Julianne, "Okay, let's start over." This is our turning point.

We start to fully communicate with each other, which makes our dancing flow much smoother and our chemistry comes back in full force. The press starts to speculate that we are dating. When you spend all day, every day with some-

187

one that beautiful, and you are dancing that close, obviously you are going to develop an attraction. Unless you are a corpse. I will say that sometimes I have those thoughts, but I have also just ended a relationship. I am thirty-two and she is nineteen. And I know that when you start to think too much, it means don't do it! In fact, I go out of my way not to and I set Julianne up with one of my friends, a Latin actor in Los Angeles.

It is my best move of the competition. She is happy and she is always in a good mood now. He comes to the rehearsals and the shows. Afterward we all go out together. Because Julianne and I are always in the same spots, the media speculation is fierce.

This is foreign territory to me. I cannot believe that people care so much about other people's love lives. Julianne is really smart about it, since she has been through it all before. "Just don't say anything," she tells me. "Don't make any comments about your ex-fiancée or you and me. This happened last year with Apolo and the best thing to do is just stay silent." I follow Julianne's lead. The paparazzi start to follow us, clicking away on their cameras and shouting questions at us. It is both crazy and pretty amusing to see it firsthand. They are jumping over each other and getting in fights to take our picture. I can't get used to it.

"This happens every season," the casting director tells me. "It's inevitable. You are always with each other and you are dancing so close, so the press will always say people are dating. It's best not to say anything." I am a little nervous about having the press speculate about us being "an item," because I have just broken off an engagement and I don't want Aliette to think I have moved on so quickly. But I keep quiet, as I have been instructed to. The truth of the matter is that I am single for the first time in quite a while. Julianne and I do get close, but it is more of a brother-sister relationship. Kati adopts her, too, so we are all together all the time. That is the way my family operates. And I don't want a relationship—I want to hit the town.

The entire cast becomes like a family over the course of those three months. We eat all of our meals together, we party together, we karaoke together. Julianne is no fun to karaoke with because her voice is too good. "No more for you," I tell her. "Just sit down and listen to the rest of us sing off tune."

Every Monday after the show, we all go out to a club called the Lounge. One night all of the cameras are outside again. A guy puts his microphone in front of me and says, "Helio, say hello to *Access Hollywood*." I can't understand what he is saying. At the time I don't even know what *Access Hollywood* is. Kati is trying to repeat it to me, but I can't hear her, either.

"Let's get out of here," I say. "This is crazy."

That night, Kati and I are relaxing at the hotel. I'm flipping through the channels looking for ballroom dancing. "Can you believe this?" I ask Kati. "Two months ago, if you told me I would be looking for ballroom dancing instead of *SportsCenter,* I would have said you were insane."

Kati goes back to Miami and a few days later calls to say she will not be able to make it to the show that Monday. She has just found out she is pregnant and she's been getting sick. It can't believe it. Only a week before we had seen some kids playing and Kati had told me, "I'm not ready to have kids yet, but I wish we had an older brother so we could have nieces and nephews."

And now she is calling me and telling me she's pregnant?

She is a little nervous about it because the IRS investigation is still ongoing and we don't know what is going to happen. "It's kind of crazy timing," she says.

"This is amazing!" I say. "It is a perfect time. With every-thing we are going through, this will keep us happy."

"You are really happy?"

"Of course! But are you going to be able to come out next week? Next week is the semifinals!"

Week eight is the first time we have to dance two dances—the paso doble and the quickstep. I have been waiting for the paso doble all season. It's the very macho "kill the bull" dance that I saw Apolo master the year before. Cindric comes out to watch that week and I am determined not to choke like I did when Roger was there. Julianne and I spend a lot of time working on the paso doble and less time on the quickstep.

By that point in the season, the media hype is tremendous. The day of the show, I wake up at four in the morning and do three hours of radio interviews; then I go to breakfast with Cindric, and then on to dress rehearsals. By four in the afternoon I have already done both dances twice. Instead of being tired, I am raring to go.

We dance the paso doble first and we do well, but we don't score as high as I hoped. The judges gave us all 9s. Then we come to the quickstep. I am much looser than I was in the paso doble. I am wearing a bright yellow suit and I'm ready to have fun. I am not overthinking it—I am excited instead of nervous. There is a big surprise moment at the end when I kiss Julianne and it is my favorite step! I cannot wait to hear the audience reaction.

It turns out to be our best dance yet. The audience and judges go nuts when we do the kiss at the end. For the first time, we score triple tens! After that dance, my phone starts to go crazy. All of these drivers are texting me, and not just from IndyCar. Guys from Nascar, Truck Series, and Sprint Car are all really into it. "That was awesome!" they are telling me. "You've got to win this thing!" Instead of making fun of me, all of the drivers are getting really competitive. Except Gil, who of course is making fun—"What is with the yellow suit?" he tells me.

The IndyCar league starts a "Vote Helio" campaign and I am getting a lot of messages through the Web site's blog. I am amazed and amped up by all the attention. Now that I know everyone is watching, I am more determined than ever to win the whole thing.

When Julianne and I make it to the finals, she pulls out all the stops. I am the only male contestant left—it is Marie Osmond, Mel B, and me. I know that I have a disadvantage because the professional men will be able to do all of the lifts that I can't do. But this is the last lap of the race and I'm ready to go full throttle. For the finals, we have to do three dances and the most important is the freestyle. In freestyle, there are no limitations and I know I am in for the biggest challenge yet. Julianne is a daredevil and I am scared of what she is going to come up with.

The day she shows me the freestyle, I walk into the studio and see a padded mat in the center of the room. I know I'm in for it. Julianne shows me this insane choreography for the freestyle. She wants me to do all of these flips and crazy lifts. For one of the lifts I have to spin her around my head—that is the most difficult one of all of them. I am not the world's strongest guy, and even though Julianne is tiny, she is all muscle.

Until the day of the show, I can't get that lift right. It is right in the middle of the dance and I am nervous about what will happen if I mess it up during the show. She calls a few of her dancing coaches and they can't help, either. "Julianne," I say, "if these guys can't do it, how am I going to?"

"Don't worry. You can do it."

We are practicing and practicing and still, no success. We have been in the studio for ten hours when I remember Apolo telling me it would be this crazy. My shoulder starts to get swollen and I finally say, "Julianne, I think we have to go for plan B."

"No, there is no plan B. You can do it."

We go to the dress rehearsal and I am so tired and sore that I really mess the lift up, almost dropping Julianne.

"Are you sure you don't want to go with a plan B?" I ask her again, sure that she will change her mind now.

"No plan B," she says.

When it's showtime and the music starts, my adrenaline kicks in just as if I'm starting at Indy. We begin really strong and when it comes time for the lift, I go for it. Magically, I do it so perfectly that I put her down two beats ahead of the game. She is coming up slowly and I'm thinking, why is she coming up so slow? Then I realize it's because I finally aced the lift. When we finish, I am jumping around and screaming, "I did it! I did it!"

Judges Len and Bruno both give us 10s. Len tells us it is the best freestyle of the night. But Carrie Ann gives us a 9 because she says there was a slight wobble on the way down from that lift. There was no wobble!

After the show I go up to Carrie Ann and joke with her. "Watch the tape, Carrie Ann! There was no wobble!" (To this day, I still joke with her about it.)

The next day is the results show and all of the Web sites are predicting that Mel B is going to win. But I know I have an army of voters behind me. Cindric has all of Team Penske voting, the Firestone Factory is voting, the Indy Racing League, the Philip Morris sponsors, and much of the racing community. I tell Julianne that we have to prepare a speech that will work for first or second. We spend half an hour coming up with the right words.

When it comes time to announce the winner, I close my eyes and Julianne and I hold hands. "And the winner is . . . Helio Castroneves and his partner, Julianne Hough!" We start to jump around. There is no fence to climb, but Kati comes out with a carton of milk. Nobody knows what she is doing until we explain the Indy tradition of drinking milk after you win.

I forget the speech Julianne and I have come up with and I just try to thank everyone I can think of—"I want to thank Team Penske, IndyCar, my family, my friends. . . ." They try to cut me off, but I keep going anyway. When they hand me the Mirrorball Trophy I have a grin across my face like I have just won the championship. I never thought I would be calling a mounted disco ball a trophy, but it is one of my most valuable wins, because it is really the first time I have stepped outside of my comfort zone and done anything besides racing. I have proved to myself that if I really work at it, I can achieve anything. Even ballroom dancing. I come away with a crazy group of new friends—Julianne, Marie Osmond, Jennie Garth, Wayne Newton, Floyd Mayweather, Mark Cuban, Cameron Mathison, Sabrina Bryan, plus all of the people behind the camera. The lighting crew, the casting crew, the hair and makeup team—we all have become a family.

We go on a media tour right after the final show and during that media tour, my ex-fiancée issues a press release announcing our broken engagement. I am shocked. This is three months after it had happened! Of course, now it looks like Julianne and I are really together and that I left my fiancée for her. Julianne and I are in New York for a few talk shows and we go out to dinner together. To us it is natural, just another dinner together as friends, but the press has a field day. They talk about us on *ET* and *Access Hollywood*—I am quite familiar with all of those shows by this time—"Julianne and Helio dance around romance talk." "Dirty Dancing between Julianne and Helio." Julianne's face is on the cover of *People* magazine with the caption underneath, "Is Julianne a Homewrecker?" I think it bothers me more than it does her. She shrugs her shoulders and says, "It doesn't matter what they think. I know the truth." Wow. I am impressed. I have to learn to be more like that, I think. Little do I know how well that skill will serve me in the following year.

When I return to Miami, I find out what Apolo was talking about when he said winning the Mirrorball Trophy was bigger than winning the gold medal. I can't even go to the grocery store anymore without getting surrounded by fans. People come up to me and thank me and tell me stories. One older woman approaches me and says, "You saved my life!"

"What? How did I do that?"

"I was going through chemo and each week for that few hours, I could take my mind off of it. You looked like you were having such a good time. Your smile was infectious."

It is such a great moment. I haven't done anything special, but this woman related to me and somehow I helped her get through a rough period in her life. I feel so blessed to have been able to impact even just one person in a positive way.

Dancing with the Stars ends on November 28, 2007, and for a week afterward, my phone goes mad—text messages, e-mails, voice mails from old friends, new friends, friends of friends. "Great job!" "You were amazing!" "I knew you could do it!" I can't believe I'm getting so much attention from a dance competition! I tease Kati: "You are the dancer and I brought home the biggest dancing trophy." I display the Mirrorball right alongside my Indy trophies—I am just as proud of it as I am of the Baby Borgs.

Part 3

Be more concerned with
your character than your
reputation, because your
character is what you really
are, while your reputation
is merely what others
think you are.

—JOHN WOODEN

CHAPTER 11

Stop, Slow Down, Go Back

**A bend in the road
is not the end of the road . . .
unless you fail to make the turn.**
—UNKNOWN

"IT SEEMS YOUR dancing has put you back on the government's radar," my lawyer tells me.

"What do you mean?"

"The IRS investigation has picked up steam. It is looking more and more likely that you will be charged with six counts of tax evasion and conspiracy."

Stop, slow down, go back.

Conspiracy? Six counts of what? What is happening? What did I do?

Kati has been aware of the details of the situation from long before when I was. I know that the IRS has been checking our files, but I have tried to make myself believe that it is just a bad dream and will all go away. Kati knows what is coming, but once again, she has kept me sheltered. I have been away racing and dancing while she has stayed in Miami dealing with attorneys and IRS agents searching through the office. When it becomes clear that the investigation is going to turn into a trial, Kati and my lawyers sit me down to explain the situation. One phrase echoes through my head: "If convicted, the worst-case scenario is five years in prison for each charge."

"Five what?" I say. "Prison?" This is not making sense to me at all. They are talking to me as though I murdered someone. As my business manager, Kati is being charged with the same counts, along with my lawyer, Alan Miller. I have no clue what we have done wrong. I have trusted Alan Miller and my accountants to handle all the tax and money issues. I know nothing about this side of the business and now I feel foolish for not paying attention to it. The lawyers ask me questions about my own company and I don't know the answers.

Alan calls me maybe ten or twelve times, trying to get me to understand what is going on. "You need more than a tax attorney. You have to hire a criminal defense attorney," he says. He gives me the number of his friend Roy Black. "He's the best guy in Miami."

"Criminal defense attorney? I'm not a criminal!"

"I know, Helio. But please. Listen to me."

In my first meetings with the lawyers, they are only telling me the negative—prison, deportation, never being able to race again. "Stop telling me the negative. Tell me something positive," I say. I point to my tax lawyer, David Garvin. "David, what is the situation?"

He tells me, "I am the best tax attorney in Florida. I have won more cases in South Florida than any other lawyer. We are going to win this case."

"Okay," I say. "Now let's focus on the positive stuff."

⨍

Every time my phone beeps, I am afraid to look at it. Nine times out of ten it is a message from my lawyers: "Can you come in to the office tomorrow?" "Do you have time for a conference call this afternoon?" But three days before the New Year, I receive a very welcome message. "Wishing you a Merry Christmas and Happy New Year! Love, Adriana." I have not heard from her in nearly two years. Why now? After so long? In any case, I am very happy to see her name on my phone now. I feel like I am on a roller coaster of emotions. Up, down, up. It has become a common pattern in my life. If I try to understand it, I will probably drive myself crazy. The trick, I learn, is to stop questioning all the time. Stop asking why and just let God's plan play itself out—it always seems to work out better than anything I have in mind anyway.

This is not to say I expect things to fall into my lap. I know that I have to take some initiative. I pick up my phone and instead of just texting back, I decide to be gentlemanly and go for a good old-fashioned phone call. "Hey, muchacha," I say with a horrible Spanish accent. "What are you doing?"

"Not much. I'm in Atlanta with my family. How about you?"

"I am in Miami."

"You are lucky. We are freezing here."

We start talking as if we have never missed a beat. "What are you doing for New Year's?" I ask her.

"Nothing, really. I'm going back to Cartagena the day after."

"Well, I'm having a New Year's Eve party. Do you want to come?"

"Sure, that sounds fun."

"You can stay at my house if you want."

"No, no, that's okay."

"You can stay with my sister."

"Thank you, but that's okay. I'll be okay. I can stay with my aunt." She is talking to me as if I'm crazy. I just think I'm being polite! Then I remember why it didn't work out the first time and I remind myself to slow down. *Slow down.*

ſ

She flies in on the thirtieth and sends me a message: "I'm going to dinner with my aunt if you want to join us. Nobu Restaurant. Eight p.m."

I text back: "For sure. See you then."

When I get to the restaurant, she gives me a funny look. "Why are you alone?" she asks.

"Who do you want me to be with?"

"Your wife! Aren't you married?"

"No. Don't you watch TV?"

"Not really. I've been away in Colombia most of the year. Did you get divorced?"

"No, it's a long story."

We catch up over dinner. I tell her about my engagement, the breakup, and *Dancing with the Stars*. She tells me that she just got out of a long-term relationship herself. She has been in Cartagena for the past few months and has not seen any of *Dancing with the Stars*. "Oh, don't worry," I tell her. "I have all the tapes."

"Wonderful," she says jokingly. "I was hoping you would say that."

After dinner we go out to a nightclub to meet up with some friends. On our way there, she tells me, "You know, I sent that text message to everybody in my phone."

"Oh. Yeah, I know that," I say. I am still not sure, though. Some part of me thinks she is trying to keep me in check and let me know that I should not start to get a big head. Whatever the case may be, I do believe that some force has brought us back together for a reason. I am not about to give up so easily this time.

The next night is New Year's Eve and I pick her up for the party at her aunt's house. Typical Miami New Year's attire is something like shorts and a hot pink minidress. Adriana comes down the stairs in a stylish white pantsuit. Very chic. Very un-Miami. Very impressive. Throughout the evening I remind myself to stay cool and go at her speed. We end up staying together the whole time, just like the party two years ago in Cartagena. At midnight, we share a New Year's kiss. When we are in the moment, I think, Okay, this is something special. I will learn to go slow for this girl.

The next few months, we keep it at a nice, comfortable pace. We speak on the phone every few days and visit each other every few weeks; there is no pressure. My lawyers demand more of my attention than Adriana! It is different from any relationship I have been in before. It is exciting, and everything is going along smoothly. There is no jealousy or mistrust. She is strong and independent, and has no time or patience to play games. When she wants to tell me something, she lets me know right away. She's a straight shooter and I like it.

May rolls around and I am in Indianapolis preparing for the race. I have not called Adriana in almost two weeks, because I was in Japan preparing for a race. I got caught up with the crazy schedule and the time difference. When I get back to the States, I finally call her. "Hey, muchacha! How are you?"

The first words she says are "What do you want from this relationship? I need to know."

"Whoa. What is going on? I thought we were going slow. I thought that is what you wanted."

"Well, if this is going to go forward, you have to act like you want me."

Man, am I crazy or what? First I am going too fast, now too slow?

I have no experience with a girl like this. In the past, I gave up on relationships when they didn't seamlessly fit into my life. But I am not willing to do that this time. I have been told that you have to change a bit for a relationship to work and I think I am finally starting to understand this. I realize that nothing is going to seamlessly fit into my life. If I want to build a stable relationship, I'll have to make adjustments in my life.

I invite her to the next race—the Milwaukee Mile, held on June 1. When a girl comes to the first race of a relationship it is a nerve-racking experience. If you crash, then what do you do? She is bad luck. You have to end it. (I'm just kidding . . . kind of.)

Thankfully, nothing bad happens. But I don't win, either. It is an average race and I come in fifth. Okay, not bad, I think. This could turn into something.

Throughout that summer, Adriana and I grow closer and I am getting the feeling that she might be "the one." All of my friends who are married tell me, "When you know you just know." For years I thought that was just an old cliché, but now I know exactly what they mean.

But I keep wondering why this is happening now. When I have this big IRS cloud looming over me? I have not yet told her about the investigation, because I am staying optimistic and praying it will go away. And yes, maybe I am a little scared that she will run away once I lay everything out on the line. How should I say it? The U.S. government is accusing me of being a criminal? It is not the easiest news to break to the woman I am trying to impress.

Racing-wise, I am having a very frustrating season. I have had a lot of second- and third-place finishes, but I have not won yet. The next race Adriana comes to is August 24 in Sonoma and it is a key race. If I win, it will put me back in the hunt for the championship. But the Wednesday before the race, as the team is en route to the track, there is a transporter fire and we lose both primary cars and a lot of our equipment. The crew rushes to build two backup cars for both Ryan and myself. It is a two-day job and they accomplish it in twelve hours, in time for us to qualify.

When I cross the finish line in first place I pump my fists as I always do. Then I run to the fence. Then I go to see my family and Adriana. Dad says right away, "You are forty-three points behind Scott Dixon." He always knows these things before anyone else. "You can make that up in the final races," he tells me. "You are back in the championship hunt!"

"All right," I say jokingly to Adriana. "You have to come to all the races now. You're a good-luck charm."

I place in second in the following race at Detroit, which puts me within thirty points of the IRL leader. I head to Chicagoland Speedway for the third-to-last race of the season. I know that I have to come in the top there to have any shot at the championship. But the points show that if Scott Dixon comes in eighth or higher, he will secure the title. I cannot control what Dixon does; all I can do is win and hope that it's enough to keep me in the fight. However, I am penalized during the qualifying round for going over the white-lined boundary and I must start in the last-place position, twenty-eighth.

I shoot to the middle of the pack within the first few laps and by the seventy-eighth lap, I have pushed my way up to the lead. Okay, I think, now I just have to stay here. I keep my cool and maintain control, though it is one of the most exciting runs of my career. During the final laps, Dixon and I are sprinting toward the checkered flag, neck and neck. We cross the line side by side and look up at the monitor to see who has won. I see Dixon's name at the top of the board and I deflate. I begin the walk toward victory lane to take my spot on the second-place podium.

Just before I make it there, an official stops me. "Helio, we checked the replay. It was a photo finish. You won by a nose." I start to jump around and hug everyone in sight.

They inform me that I came across .0033 seconds before Dixon, the second-closest margin in the history of IndyCar. Though I know that Dixon has secured the championship with his second-place finish, I am still overjoyed by such a thrilling victory. To go from last to first, to have a team behind me that refused to quit, and to win by a hundredth of a second—it is an exhilarating moment. I have proven to myself just why I can never, ever give up.

Adriana's birthday is September 17 and luckily I have a race in Atlanta in the upcoming weeks. I fly there to practice and to celebrate with her. Her family throws her a big party and I meet everyone all at once—her sisters, aunts, uncles, cousins, friends. It is a must-not-crash situation! They are all just like Adriana: funny, kind, but no-nonsense. You can tell if they like you or not right away. They are not going to be fake for you. Thank goodness, I pass the test. I get along with everyone without any awkward or uncomfortable situations. Phew! I feel like things are really falling into place.

But then a few days after the party, my lawyer, Roy, calls with really bad news. "You are going to be indicted this Friday," he says.

"What does this mean? What is our next step?"

"The formal indictment will come on Friday. You have to be in Miami on Friday morning to turn yourself in to the IRS."

My stomach sinks to the floor.

I am confused, upset, and preoccupied. How am I going to tell Adriana? How am I going to tell Roger? "Am I going to miss my race?" I want to know.

"When is it?"

"On Saturday, October fourth. It's in Atlanta."

"You should be okay. You should be able to get back that Friday night."

"Can't we do it earlier, so I can make it back in time to practice?"

"No, unfortunately. I've already tried, but the prosecution says they cannot have their documents ready any earlier."

What a mess. And what horrible timing. Now I have to tell Adriana. I have just met her whole family. I made a really good first impression, and now this? They are going to think I'm some kind of criminal!

When I break the news to her, I expect her to get upset or anxious, but she barely flinches. "Don't worry," she says. "I'm sure it will be fine." I wonder if she is just being nice. The first chance she gets, I am sure she is going to make her escape. And I can't say I'd blame her.

Then I call Roger and tell him what is going to happen. "Okay," he tells me, as calm as can be. "You take care of what you have to take care of. Don't worry about the race."

But of course I'm worried about the race. I'm worried about everything. How is everyone staying so calm?

I spend the week in Atlanta, preparing for the Petit Le Mans. On Thursday I fly back to Miami for the indictment. Adriana drives me to the airport and when she drops me off, she tells me again, "Don't worry. It will be fine. I'll pick you up here tomorrow night and it will all be over."

CHAPTER 12

Losing Control

**That which does not kill me
makes me stronger.**
—FRIEDRICH NIETZSCHE

FRIDAY MORNING, KATI and I stand in my kitchen with our parents, holding hands and praying. At seven we leave for the courthouse. We are prepared to plead not guilty, appear before the judge, and be home within a few hours so I can jump on another plane back to Atlanta.

At eight in the morning Kati and I surrender to the IRS office. The agents separate us from each other and tell us that we are not allowed to have our attorneys. Kati goes with the female agents and I go with the men. They begin asking lots of questions. What is my name? My address? Am I married? They take our pictures and then put us in handcuffs. "I'm sorry," they say. "We have to do this." We are then transferred to the federal courthouse. When we get into the elevator, we see Alan Miller. He is also in handcuffs and standing with two marshals on either side of him. Kati begins to cry. "It doesn't make sense," she says. "They are treating us like we killed someone."

They walk us down the halls, past all the IRS offices. "This is humiliating," I tell Alan.

"It's called the perp walk," Alan tells me. "It is meant to humiliate you. Just keep your head up."

Once we get to the courthouse, the marshals remove our handcuffs and put shackles on our feet. Then they lead us to our holding cells. Kati goes off to the women's side and I can no longer see her. The marshals put me in a cell by myself on the men's side. "You are going to be kept alone due to safety concerns regarding your high profile," the marshal tells me. I sit on the floor and try to fight back tears. The shackles cut into my ankles and I shift to try to find a position that is more comfortable. It is incredibly cold in the cell and I don't like being alone. I would rather have somebody to talk to. I keep looking over toward the women's side and wondering how my sister is doing. What have we done to deserve this?

A few minutes later, I see Kati passing by my cell. She looks at me and flashes her smile. When Kati smiles, she smiles with her whole face. She has these almond-shaped brown eyes that sparkle and it makes you think everything is going to be okay. But I can tell she has been crying, too. I know that right now she is staying strong for me. She has always been in control of her emotions when she needs to, while I am an open book. If I am upset, it is all over my face. Seeing Kati in the shackles makes me tear up all over again, but I fight it back. If she is going to stay strong for me, I vow to do the same for her. She begins to joke. "Hey, Helio!" she calls. "I'm making friends in my cell!"

And of course, in typical Kati style, she really is making friends. The other girls show her how to put toilet paper between the shackles so they don't cut her skin. They trade stories of what they are in for—mortgage fraud, immigration issues, and real estate scams. One girl, a Brazilian, has been stuck there for two months. She came over by boat and nobody had let her talk to the consulate. This makes Kati angry and she goes into big-sister mode, advising the girl how she has to demand an attorney and insist on speaking to the consulate.

Back in my cell, it is a bit lonelier. And by this point I am frozen. "Why is it so cold?" I ask the marshal.

"They keep it really cold to make sure everybody stays calm."

Really? Because it makes me go crazy. As the day goes on, more and more men are brought in and put in the other two cells. I am still alone in the third cell. There is no clock and I can't tell if we have been there for one hour or five hours. When the marshals bring me a tray of lunch, I assume it is about noon. I have no appetite and I take the tray and set it next to me, but don't touch anything. Soon after, the marshals switch shifts and one of the new ones starts putting the new guys in the cell with me. A four-hundred-pound man enters the cell and stands over me. My God, I think, now I'm going to die in here. The guy points at my sandwich and asks, "Are you going to eat that?"

"No, no." I hand him the tray. "It's yours. It's all yours. Take the sandwich, take the milk, take it all."

He looks at me a moment. "Hey, you're that race car driver, aren't you?"

"Yes."

"Oh man, you're all over the news. Your picture, your house, everything."

That's just great. This day just gets worse and worse.

Then one of the marshals starts yelling into the cell from the loudspeaker. "What is going on here? Everybody out of this cell!" We all go running for the door, but they scream at me, "Not you, Mr. Castroneves! You get back in there!" They move everyone else out of my cell and stuff them into the other two. They are all packed in tight. If they find a way out of those cells, for sure they are going to kill me.

Finally we are all taken to see the judge. They shackle us in groups and lead us into the elevator. I am shackled with Kati, Alan, and two other people. I see the hallway clock—it is one-thirty. I should be at practice in Atlanta right now.

"There is a lot of media out there," one of the marshals says.

"Oh no," one of the women says. "I don't want my picture taken! I don't have my makeup on."

"They are not here for you; they are here for him." The marshal points at me.

"Oh really? Who are you? Are you famous?"

I want to melt into the ground.

They bring us into the cold, sterile courtroom. Kati and I are shackled with two other siblings and two drug dealers. When we enter, I see that the room is packed and the press is there—I am surprised because I didn't know the media would be allowed in the courtroom. "These are all report-ers," I tell Kati. "I recognize a lot of them."

We see our lawyers again and I bring up the media pres-ence in the courtroom.

"Yeah. The prosecution tipped off all of this press," David tells me. "Now we know why they wanted to wait until today. It is not because they didn't have the documents ready. It's because they wanted to give the press enough warning so they would all be here today."

We are seated in the jury box and the judge begins to call people up one by one. There are mostly accused drug dealers and thieves and I am thinking that we don't belong here.

Kati and Alan are near me. Alan reminds us to be strong and not to cry, because that is exactly what the press and the government want. Of course, the more I try to stop myself, the harder it is. Kati is a concrete wall. As much as I am falling apart, she is holding it together. At one point I am visibly fighting back tears and a man sitting at the prosecu-tion table takes my picture with his camera phone. Kati gets really angry. "Hey! Hey!" she yells at him.

"It's okay, Kati," I say. "Leave it alone."

"No! He can't do that!" It is just as though we are on the racetrack and somebody has slighted me. She calls out to the closest marshal, "Excuse me, this man just took a picture of my brother with his phone. Is that allowed? Make him erase it!"

The marshal is really angry. "You are an attorney," he tells the man. "What are you doing?"

Kati points her finger at the guy and says to the marshal, "Keep an eye on this one."

The marshal smiles at Kati. "I'm sure you'll be fine. Everything will be okay. And when this is all over, everyone will want a picture with you guys."

"Of course," Kati says. "I will make sure of it!"

I am still trying to calm my nerves, which is much harder to do in a courtroom than on a track. Meanwhile, Kati is negotiating how she will get a picture with this marshal and is staring down the prosecutor. "You're crazy," I tell her. "Forget about him."

Finally it is our turn. Still in cuffs and shackles, we stand before the judge, waiting to hear our bail and bond conditions. This is the low point for me. I am humiliated to be standing in front of a judge with shackles on my feet and handcuffs around my wrists while an entire courtroom full of people looks on. Luckily the judge is a very reasonable man. He sets our conditions—we have to post bail and cannot travel outside the United States—then we are sent back to the holding cells as the lawyers handle all the paperwork. They put up my assets as collateral and surrender all of my travel documents.

As they work out the logistics, Kati and I wait in our cells. Hours pass by and we are the last ones left. I am sure they are going to leave us there. When they eventually come to release us, my attorneys tell me that there is a whole army of press waiting for me outside the main door of the court-house. "You don't have to talk to them," they explain. "Most clients don't. We can go out this side door and avoid the whole thing."

"No," I say. "I have nothing to hide. I'll talk to them." I step outside and walk down the block to the waiting micro-phones with Kati right behind me. The hardest part is com-posing myself. "I will treat this as a race," I say. I can barely make my voice come out. "It is going to be a difficult race, but I know that I did nothing wrong. I am going to rely on my attorneys and accountants and pray for justice."

When we get back to my house, my family is waiting there. We have each other to lean on and we allow ourselves to breathe after hours of agony. I have enough time to compose myself before hopping on a plane back to Atlanta. My girlfriend, Adri-ana, is supposed to pick me up at the airport. During the plane ride I keep wondering, My God, is she even going to be there? We have only been dating a few months. And now my face and my house have been splashed all over the news. She doesn't have to put up with this, I think. I have just met her family and am imagining them all telling her to stay away. And truly, I will not blame her for running in the other direction.

I land in Atlanta and as I walk to the baggage claim, I see her from a distance. As I get closer, her big brown eyes meet mine and a strong, confident smile spreads across her face. She hugs me and whispers, "You are going to be fine."

There is no time to practice, so we drive straight to the hotel. I meet Cindric in the hallway. He looks at me and asks, "Do you still want to do this?"

"Of course," I say. I know that racing is the only thing that will make me feel normal again. It is the only thing that will allow me to be in control of something.

The following morning, I go to the track early. Everyone is telling me, "It's going to be fine. You are going to come out of this without a scratch." They smile and pat me on the back, but at the same time I have the feeling that they are holding me at arm's length.

We have a team meeting in the team transporter, where there are flat-screen monitors set up to make sure everyone is in tune with the live races. We are talking and discussing strategy when suddenly everyone falls silent. I look around. What happened? I turn and see myself on TV, in handcuffs and walking to the courthouse. Nobody knows what to say, so I casually joke, "Look, I am on CNN! Wow!" But still, it's embarrassing and upsetting.

I just keep telling myself, Focus. You just have to finish this race.

My teammate, Ryan Briscoe, won the pole for us the day before, so we are starting in top position. The Petit Le Mans is an overnight race and I am worried about having to drive through the night. The race starts at 11 a.m. and is supposed to finish late at night. By late afternoon I still have not been called to race. I tell Roger that I don't want to drive at night, because I haven't practiced.

"Okay, no problem," Roger says.

Then, as dusk is falling, he turns to me and says, "Okay, Helio, you're up. Let's go." I get in the car and I can't see much of anything. Everything is shifting around me. I chant to myself: Focus. Focus. Focus. The Petit Le Mans is a grueling ten-hour race, but for me it's a glorious period of time when everything else fades away; I forget about what has just happened in Miami. Roger is making great tactical calls and I am out in the front for much of the race. He keeps telling me to slow down and just worry about finishing. At that point, slowing down is the last thing I want to do. I have to shake the past twenty-four hours from my mind and the only way I know how is to hurl myself forward as fast as possible. I don't slow down until I cross the finish line. For the first time in days, I am where I belong.

When I stand on the podium, the reporters ask me how I did it. How did I go from a jail cell to the top of the podium in a matter of twenty-four hours? It is a crazy question to me. "This is who I am," I answer. "This is all I know how to do."

Since I was eleven years old, my life has been based on this forward quest. *Look ahead, go faster, just drive.* But the next day I know I am headed back to Miami, where everything will begin to play in reverse. It scares the hell out of me.

∫

On October 10, I appear before the judge to ask him for permission to go to Australia for the last race of the Indy-Car season. It is the same judge and the same courtroom as the bail hearing, though this time the room is not nearly as crowded. I see the main prosecutor, Matt Axelrod, for the first time. Though I know he was at the bail hearing, I don't recall seeing him; that entire day was a blur. This time I stay calm and focused. I study Axelrod and his image imprints itself on my mind. He is exactly what I would imagine a federal agent to look like—tall, broad-shouldered, slightly hunched over, hair in a severe side part. He wears a stuffy suit and an intense gaze. The moment I hear him talk, I realize he has made up his mind and will do anything to win this case.

"This man is a criminal." He points at me. "You cannot let him leave the country. He will flee."

The blood rushes to my head. Who is this guy? He doesn't know me. We have never spoken; we have never even made eye contact before this moment, yet he holds his finger in my face and repeats, "This man is a criminal. He will flee."

The judge addresses me. "Mr. Castroneves, I understand that you raced in Atlanta this past Saturday? The day after the indictment."

"Yes, your honor."

"And did you win?"

"Yes, your honor."

"That is pretty impressive, Mr. Castroneves."

"Thank you."

"I will tell you one thing. The prosecutor is doing his job by saying that you are a flight risk. However, I choose not to believe him in this matter. What you did this past weekend is remarkable. It proves that you are very good at what you do. I don't think you are willing to risk your career by fleeing. However, if you do, then we are going to find you, and you are going to dance with the marshals."

"I understand, your honor. And I will bring you the trophy."

However, I don't win the race in Australia. That would have been too perfect. I come in seventh and return to Miami, without a trophy, set to prepare for the biggest race of my life.

I know that the next six months will be a constant backward journey of s*top, slow down, go back.*

CHAPTER 13

Preparation

**Be patient and tough; someday this
pain will be useful to you.**

—OVID

I T IS NOVEMBER 2008. My parents, Kati, Eduardo, and baby Eduardo move into my home. I don't want to be alone. In this moment, the big house, the fancy cars, and all of the trophies are meaningless. I want my family around. I need them there for support. I want everyone to be together so we can stay strong for each other. It is not easy for any of us—we all feel helpless and confused. When Adriana moves in, I am so thankful. She gives me the support that I need. "It will be fine," she keeps saying. We are both aware that this may not be the case, but just hearing her say it puts my mind at ease. If she can stick through this, I think, she can stick through anything. Day and night is spent in preparation for my trial. And now we have a whole new cast of characters joining us.

David Garvin, my tax attorney. Cheerful, sharp, and very smart. He knows the tax codes like the palm of his hand. Tall, with eyeglasses, and the look of a biology teacher. I guess that's how a tax attorney should look.

Roy Black, my criminal attorney. He is very sociable, caring, and fatherly. But when it comes to the case, he is a warrior and a legal mastermind. He has an impressive reputation and incredible court presence.

The Srebnick brothers represent Kati. The older brother, Howard, is funny and charismatic. He looks more like Jon

Bon Jovi than Perry Mason. Scotty, the younger brother, is a walking encyclopedia of the law, with a degree from Harvard Law and a federal court clerkship pedigree.

Alan Miller, my business attorney, who is also being charged with tax evasion and conspiracy. A strong, broad-shouldered former NFL player. There is not a bad bone in his body.

Bob Bennett, Alan's attorney and formerly Bill Clinton's attorney. A roly-poly, incredibly smart, incredibly funny man. Has a fondness for purple suspenders and purple ties. If this is a race, he is the race adviser. He knows what we need to do in terms of strategy and preparation.

I know that I have a great team. Still, it is the most grueling off-season of my life. For five straight months, I prepare for the trial with my lawyers and Kati. They come over to my house almost every night. When I prepare for a race, I know what to do, what to expect, and how to react. When we begin preparations for the trial, I am lost. Not only am I confused by the charges that are being brought against me, but I'm also baffled by the trial process, the legal system, and American tax codes. The more the lawyers explain it to me, the more confused I become. The more questions they ask me, the more I realize I don't know the answers to key elements of my life.

In what year did my father form Seven?

Not sure.

Do I know why $5 million of my money is sitting in an account in the Netherlands?

No.

Roughly how much money did my father invest in my career?

A lot. You want a number? I can't even begin to guess.

Do I know how much money I have in my bank account?

No clue.

For me, we are not just preparing for trial; I am receiving an education in the side of my life I never touched—the business side. Kati takes over when they ask most of the financial questions. My father flies in from Brazil to explain everything in detail to the lawyers. I struggle to make sense of the words and figures they are throwing about every day.

One night, we all go out to dinner—my lawyers, my parents, Alan, Kati, Adriana, and myself. I am frustrated that I still cannot understand the case. They are repeating those same terms again: "constructive receipts" and "deferred payment."

I bang my fist on the table. "You keep saying these words but I have no idea what you mean! Will somebody please explain to me in simple terms what the hell you are talking about?"

David takes a dollar out of his wallet and sets it on the table. "You see this dollar? I am going to give you this dollar. You have a choice to make here. If you want to take it now, I will take out the forty percent of taxes you owe on it and give you sixty cents."

"Okay."

"But if you want to put it in the Fintage licensing firm in the Netherlands for ten years, this dollar will earn interest and grow to be ten dollars. But you can't touch it. You defer payment on it."

"Okay."

"Now, at the end of that five years, I will still only tax you on this dollar I am giving you right now. So you can take the money now, which leaves you with sixty cents. Or you can take the money later, which leaves you with nine dollars and sixty cents. Which do you want to do?"

"Well, obviously I want the nine sixty."

"Right, so that is why you put the dollar in the Fintage account. That is why Alan put your money in the Fintage account. Except it wasn't a dollar. It was five million dollars. So imagine how much interest you stand to make by deferring payment on that five million dollars for ten years."

"A lot, I guess."

"Yes, a lot. Nobody was trying to cheat anybody. Alan was trying to give you a retirement fund. Normal people get a 401(k), but athletes don't. He was trying to protect you. Do you understand it now?"

"I think so."

"Listen, in 2000 he put your money in Fintage for ten years so that it could collect interest for you. And in October 2009, you will have access to it, which means you will 'constructively receive' it. And then you will pay the taxes on it."

"Wait, so I am on trial for money I can't even touch yet?"

"Now you've got it, my man."

Well, that's just wonderful.

⌇

The following Saturday, Kati and I meet Howard at a Cuban cafeteria for an early-morning café con leche. I want to talk about cycling instead of trial preparations. We discuss drafting, accelerating, momentum, speed, concepts that I can relate to.

Before we leave, Howard tells me he's going to attend a bar mitzvah that morning and will work on the case in the afternoon.

"What is the purpose of the bar mitzvah?" I ask him. "I've always wondered."

"It's when a Jewish boy reaches the age of thirteen and becomes a man."

"Sort of like Confirmation?"

"Yeah, sort of," he says.

"You are Jewish?"

"Yeah."

"Are you religious?"

"I believe in the family values that Judaism promotes, but I have a lot of questions."

"Like what?"

"I could never understand the story of Abraham and Isaac. Why would God ask Abraham to sacrifice Isaac in order to prove his love for Him?"

"But in the end, God didn't let Abraham kill Isaac," I tell Howard. "God stopped him."

"But God still asked Abraham to kill his own son. What kind of God would ask a father to do that?"

"I don't have an answer for you, Howard. But I trust that there was a reason. I have faith in God's plan."

ſ

When I am told that I am going to be indicted by a "grand jury," I ask my legal team, "What the heck is a grand jury?"

"Twenty-three citizens from the community that have listened to the government's theory of the case," they explain. "You have no right to present any evidence to the grand jury and no right to have your lawyers address the grand jury. It is a totally one-sided process. As long as a majority of the grand jurors believe that there is some probability that a crime was committed and that you were involved, they can indict you and then you are forced to defend yourself in a court of law."

"Don't we get a chance to make our case to the grand jury?" I ask.

"No, the law doesn't allow your attorneys to meet or speak to the grand jurors."

"That sounds unfair. Not even with a judge supervising?"

"There is no judge in the grand jury chamber when the government presents its case to the grand jurors. The only people allowed to meet with the grand jury are the prosecutor and its witnesses."

"What do you mean there is no judge? Who makes sure that the prosecutor is presenting the case fairly and accurately?"

"The prosecutor."

"What do you mean, 'the prosecutor'? The prosecutor is the one who is trying to put me and my sister in jail. How can it be that he is the one who decides what will be presented to the grand jury? And we have no right to make sure the prosecutor is playing fair?"

"Welcome to the federal criminal justice system."

ſ

In December my lawyers start to prepare my witnesses. They ask me to compile a list of friends and colleagues who will be able to reveal my true character to the jury. We ask my old racing coach, Alfredo, to testify. When I call him, he acts strangely and tells me that he is having financial problems. He is silent for a few long moments and then I understand that he needs money to cover more than just the expenses of the trip.

"I am sorry, but I am asking for a favor," I say. "We pay for your airfare and hotel room."

"I am sorry, but it will be hard for me to leave here for two days. I have to get my visa, and my business. . . ." He continues to tell me why he cannot come. I know that he is worried—people don't want to mess with matters dealing with the government. Still, I am unbelievably hurt.

"Outside of your family, who knows you best?" the lawyers ask. "Who can tell your story from childhood all the way until now?"

"Well, my friend Tony." Meaning Tony Kanaan. "But I doubt he will do it. We've had a falling-out."

We have not spoken since that controversial race in Chicago, a year and a half ago.

I call him anyway. "Tony, I need a favor . . ."

"Of course, Helio," he tells me. "I'll be there." I am surprised. I guess I completely misjudged him.

My lawyers interview Tony and decide he will be a great guy to have on the stand—he will be able to tell who I really am.

Americo Teixeira, my first publicist; Mark Seiden, my friend and lawyer; Raul Seabra, Amir Nasr, Marina and Jose Salles, Renata and Heloisa, Edu Homem de Mello, Aleteia, Jose Maria, my mother, and my father all agree to take the stand as well. But many others essentially tell me, "I wish you the best of luck, man, but I can't do it."

A part of me understands. The IRS is a scary thing—especially to a non-U.S. citizen. Nobody wants to tango with them—believe me, I know. Still, for a friend, I would do it. It is one of those moments when I find out who my friends really are. I feel isolated and abandoned.

Christmas comes and we try to act normal for a day. We have a tree and we prepare the traditional Christmas dinner, but the spirit is not there and we all know it. We only buy presents for baby Edu—though he is six months old and too young to open them anyway. But thank God for him. He is such a smiling, happy baby. He provides light and laughter in an otherwise melancholy home. We don't celebrate New Year's Eve, which is usually one of my favorite times. But this

December 31, we know that the coming year will not bring a new beginning. We must live through a nightmare before anything can begin again.

On the weekends, Kati and I go to Howard's house to prepare for the trial. The first weekend we are there, Howard's wife, Sharon, comes out with a plate of arroz con pollo. Sharon is tall, blond, and beautiful. But she is not Latin and I am leery of this arroz con pollo. I take a plate to be polite and prepare myself. On the first bite, I look to Kati in disbelief. It is the best I have ever tasted. How is this possible?

"I grew up in Miami," Sharon tells me. "You don't think I know how to cook Latin food?"

I like her instantly.

When so many of our friends have stopped calling, e-mailing, and texting, Howard and Sharon pick up the slack. We become siblings—we spend our weekends together, we adopt each other's religions, and if I need to talk to someone at three in the morning, I dial their number.

ſ

In early January, Penske informs me that the Australian driver Will Power will fill in for me until I return. I understand the decision. I know it is business, not personal. I've seen *The Godfather*. Still, the news unnerves me. My trial is set to begin on March 2 and the season begins on April 5. I realize that is too risky for the Penske Corporation to hope that everything will be over by then. If I've learned anything about business in my racing career, it is that a successful corporation doesn't function on hope.

I fly to Indianapolis for the press conference announcing Will as the interim driver. I have to make a statement and I have it carefully prepared: "It's a bit strange to be in this situation," I begin. "But one thing I have to say is that Roger and

Tim have backed me up all the way. It's pretty good to have friends like that first of all, and also to have an organization behind me." A reporter from ESPN comments about how I am facing thirty-five years in prison. What? Where did he get his facts? Is that true? My lawyers have only told me ten! I calm myself and repeat the words I have practiced.

"My life is about racing. I feel very confident that this thing will be over soon and I'll be back in the race car doing what I love most."

CHAPTER 14

A Time of Trial

There is a higher court than
the court of justice and
that is the court of conscience.
It supersedes all other courts.
—MAHATMA GANDHI

I T IS MARCH 4, 2009, the first day of the trial. My lawyers tell Adriana not to come to the courthouse. I want to know why not.

"She is too pretty. The jurors may not like it."

"Oh." I forgot about the jurors. I begin to stress at the thought of the jury inspecting my every move. When we arrive at the courthouse, a swarm of press is outside. Kati and I walk in side by side. "Keep your head up," she tells me through smiling teeth.

Kati is sitting next to me, forcing a smile, telling me it will be okay. Dad and Mom are in the back of the courtroom. Dad is stoic. Mom cries and prays.

∫

The trial begins like a race. We stand in front of an American flag, we listen to announcements, I hear my name called, the judge instructs the lawyers to begin. And the flag drops.

The first few laps are bumpy. The government attorney, Matt Axelrod, delivers his opening statement. He points at me several times and calls me a criminal. A villain who planned to defraud the U.S. government. And he points at Kati and Alan, calling them coconspirators in my plan. I begin to panic. I remind myself to calm down. The race is long. There will be time to show everyone what I am really made of.

My attorneys present their opening statements, explaining the real story. I am not a criminal mastermind, they tell the jury, but rather a race car driver who knows nothing of U.S. tax law or even my own finances. All my life, that has been out of my line of vision. As my attorneys set the record straight, I feel much better about my chances.

The hardest part for me is that the government gets to present its case first. For weeks, the prosecutors paint me as a criminal. In the simplest terms, this is their story: In 1999, I signed a licensing deal with Penske for $5 million. Immediately after I signed, they claimed that Kati, Alan Miller, and I conspired to find a way to get out of paying taxes on that money. Alan sent $5 million to a company in the Netherlands, Fintage. This was done so the government couldn't get its hands on any of that money. There was also a $2 million sponsorship I had with Coimex, and this money was sent to Seven Promotions, a shell company in Panama, a company I owned. This is the way they tell the tale. Their first witness is the Panamanian man who formed Seven Panamanian. I've never met him before.

On the second day of trial, Larry Bluth, the general counsel for Penske Racing, takes the stand. In front of him there is a stack of papers—a driver contract, a licensing agreement, a relationship agreement, a promotional representation agreement—the same stack of papers I signed at a suite in the Dearborn Inn nearly ten years ago.

"The driver contract is twenty-one pages long, is it not?" my attorney, Roy Black, asks.

"Yes," Bluth responds.

"And it's single-spaced and full of legal language, isn't it?"

"It's single-spaced and full of legal language."

"Yes. Well, let me ask you about some of these things. It's fairly complicated stuff, isn't it?"

"It could be complicated."

"Well, it is complicated, is it not?" Roy asks.

"It depends on the reader."

"Well, you think somebody, a twenty-four-year-old young man from Brazil, not learned in the law, could read this in an hour and understand it?"

The prosecutor, Matt Axelrod, stands up. "Objection, Your Honor." A cell phone rings.

"One moment," the judge says. "Just a moment. A little music to keep us awake here. Perfect timing, as a matter of fact."

Light laughter ripples through the courtroom. I shift in my chair.

"Objection, Your Honor," Axelrod says again.

"Sustained."

Roy continues: "Let me ask you to look at paragraph twelve-point-zero-one of the driver agreement." Bluth flips through the stack and Roy starts to read from his own papers.

Roy has the look of a lawyer. Short, gray hair, wire-rimmed glasses, tall and intimidating presence. When he speaks, I am not sure I catch everything he says. I get lost in the legal language. Throughout the trial, I continually lean over and whisper to Howard, Kati's lawyer, "Howie, what's going on now?" Kati pushes me back and says, "Hey, you have two law-yers. Howard is mine. Leave him alone."

Roy is still talking. ". . . if this Agreement shall have been executed with the invalid portion thereof eliminated and it is thereby declared the intention of the parties hereto . . ."

I lean to Howard. "What the hell is he talking about?"

"He is reading from your Penske contracts," he tells me.

"Oh." I have never read it.

It is only the second day of the trial and I am already exhausted. It is 4 p.m. and I have been sitting in this chair since 8 a.m., trying to pay attention. But terms like "force majeure" and "Delaware corporation" float around me and I begin to check out. I look to the stack of papers and then Larry Bluth and then to Kati. My mind flashes back to the suite in the Dearborn Inn, November 5, 1999. I was a twenty-four-year-old kid, overjoyed to be signing those contracts with Penske; I thought it was the greatest day of my life. If I had known that it would have led to this trial, would I have read through those contracts instead of just signing them? Would I have corrected all the mistakes? I am not sure I would have even known where to start.

ſ

In order to present the real story, my lawyers don't begin in 1999. They go all the way back to my boyhood in Ribeirão Preto, when I first began racing go-karts. They tell of my father's determination, my family's dedication, and then the family bankruptcy. They tell how my father's lawyer had set up Seven Promotions for him, so that my father could protect his assets and find sponsors for me. This was all done because Emerson was not doing his job; furthermore, he was taking the commissions on any sponsorships that Kati or my dad had secured. My father had to find a way to stop this from happening—this was the best way he knew how. It was set up in Panama because the Brazilian bank had a lien on all of my father's properties, so he could not set up a company in Brazil under his own name. The money would have been taken right away. And the $2 million Coimex sponsorship that the defense spoke of was really a $200,000 sponsorship, of which I received only $50,000, which I did pay taxes on. The other $150,000 went to Seven, not to get out of paying taxes, but to pay for my expenses that year. Whatever money remained would be to pay my father back for the years of work he had done for me, and the millions of dollars he had spent. This was the very beginning of what I owed back to him.

They tell of the terrible Greg Moore crash in 1999, and how when I signed with Penske, Kati and I were jumping up and down on our hotel beds, so excited to have a three-year deal that the money was an afterthought. I would have raced for free just to have the security of a three-year deal. My lawyers ask if anybody honestly thinks for a second that midway through we stopped jumping, looked at Alan Miller, and said, "Let's figure out a way to defraud the U.S. government." And does anybody think that Alan, who was still grieving the death of Greg Moore, a driver to whom he was so close that he named his son after him, said, "Okay, let's do it. I am willing to gamble my life and my reputation for this." Really? Does that make any sense to anybody in the courtroom?

It takes weeks to lay out both sides of the story. Nearly a month into the trial, I am not certain which side is leading the field. I am tired, scared, and baffled by the entire process. My mind is about to explode. There is too much going on around me. I am being called a criminal on a daily basis. I have just recently found the person I want to spend the rest of my life with, yet we cannot move forward—we must stay in standby mode. I see my parents suffering, having both their son and daughter in such a position. I see my sister, who just had a baby and is not able to be with him, instead sitting in this courtroom with me on trial for my taxes. How did she get drawn into this? I know that the only thing I know how to do is race—and that may well be taken from me. The world is spinning and I feel my identity slipping away.

I remind myself that God has a plan, though what it is, I'm not clear of at this moment. Is it for me to go to jail and come out even stronger? Is it to draw me closer to those I love? Is it to make me aware of how blessed I am? Is it to test my faith? One thing I am sure of: I am not going to lose faith. I repeatedly look to a quote written in my notebook— "Faith is to see the invisible, believe in the incredible, and receive the impossible." I remind myself to see, believe, and receive whatever it is that God has in store.

ſ

Every morning of the trial, I wake up at five-thirty. Kati, my parents, and I go to 6 a.m. mass at Epiphany Church near my home. When Kati kisses little Eduardo, her nine-month-old son, good-bye, my heart has pangs. I know that they have brought Kati into this trial because they thought I would plea bargain to save her from the ordeal. Early on, they made an offer—if I pled guilty, they would let her go. With her being a new mother, they thought this would pressure me into a plea bargain. She would have no part of it. "No way," she has told me. "You are not pleading guilty to anything. We have done nothing wrong. We are in this together." I am amazed at her strength. "It was my job to take care of your business affairs. I did the best I could. If mistakes were made, and someone is going to go to jail, it's going to be me, not you." Clearly the U.S. government grossly underestimated her.

As we all sit in the pew, we hold hands. I talk to God. "Dear Lord, whatever your plan is for me, I can accept it. But please, keep my family safe. I trust in You. I believe in You."

Afterward, my father drives us to the courthouse and Kati and I sit on the curb outside, waiting for it to open. We always arrive at least twenty minutes early—I want to be sure we are on time. As we sit there together, I wonder how it came to this. I have worked so hard for so long to achieve the great American dream. And Kati has dedicated her life to helping me get there. We have been on a roller coaster together. Born into a very fortunate childhood, we suffered through years of family bankruptcy. We celebrated each turn of destiny and leaned on each other at every bump in the road. And now we are two immigrant kids sitting on a bench outside a courthouse, hoping for American justice.

243

∫

Each afternoon, when we arrive home from court, Adriana says, "Let's go for a bike ride." We ride around the streets of my neighborhood and try to talk about everything but the trial. When I haven't slept for weeks, she tells me, "You know they can't really send you to jail for ten years. Your lawyers are being sensational."

"Are you sure?" I ask.

"Yes, I am sure. Stop worrying so much." She is lying, but it calms me down all the same. I start sleeping through the night for the first time since the trial began. I begin to realize that she has come back into my life at the exact right moment. She is keeping me strong and positive.

"When this is over," I tell her, "we are going to get married and start a family. If we can get through this, we can get through anything."

At night, the attorneys gather at my house and we prepare for the next day in court. The attorneys are not only studious and intelligent, but they are surprisingly fun to be around. Kati and I get a real kick out of Bob Bennett, a celebrity in his own right, having represented Bill Clinton in the Monica Lewinsky trial. He has such a disarming sense of humor, willing to get a laugh at his own expense. When the government accuses me of failing to pay taxes on the Hugo Boss apparel I was given as part of our team's sponsorship, Bennett jokingly pirouettes in front of the jury—an impressive move for a portly man—and complains that Hugo Boss doesn't make a suit that fits his "full-figured physique."

Kati and I grow very close to Howard. Whenever we have questions, we turn to him. When we are scared, confused, or feeling low, he will reassure us: "The truth will come out and justice will be done." Or he will launch into a joke: "So this guy is sitting at a restaurant and he orders a bowl of soup. . . ." Just hearing the beginning of it makes us start to smile. Or he will remind us that others have it worse than we do. His sister's seven-year-old son, Luke, was diagnosed with cancer at age three and has been on and off chemo for four years. "My sister worries every night whether Luke will be okay."

"God willing, he will be cured," I tell him.

"Why would God let him get so sick in the first place?" he asks me.

Late one night, I go into Kati's room. "Kati," I whisper. "Are you awake?"

"No."

"I can't sleep."

"Helio, leave me alone." She hands me her phone. "Here, call Howard."

I dial his cell number and he picks up. "Helinho," he says. "What's up!"

"I can't sleep."

He tells me about a case he and Roy tried just a couple of years earlier where they represented Howard's childhood friend, Raphael. He was indicted for laundering $8 million of drug money for the Colombian cartel. "Raphael was also a very religious man, like you, Helinho. And I would ask him, 'Why would God let you be indicted for a crime you didn't commit?' He always said to me, 'God rules the world.' Like you often say, Helinho, God has a plan."

"What happened to Raphael?"

"He was acquitted by the jury on all counts"

"See, your friend was right, Howard. God has a plan. Good night."

Every day, Roger calls me and asks how it is going. I explain it to him the only way I know how, in racing terms. "We had a good pit stop; I think we are about a lap up." "We hit a bit of dirty air today; we're a few cars behind."

"It's all about the finish line," he tells me. "Just relax. Your car is waiting for you when this is over." I feel settled after each time I talk to him.

ſ

On March 18, my former accountant, Pat Bell, testifies as a witness for the government. I feel as though we have hit the dividing wall.

He goes on and on, explaining to the court how he met with me a dozen times, and explaining my taxes. I met with him only once, and then Kati took over. He says that Kati never informed him that the money was sent to my father's company to pay him back and therefore was not to be taxed. Meanwhile, there are e-mails and correspondence to the contrary. I fume as I listen to him deny the truth.

It comes down to the final days. I know that so much depends on my last four witnesses: Tony Kanaan; Mark Seiden, my friend and former attorney; Americo Teixeira, my first publicist from when I was fourteen years old; and Helio Phydias Zeiglitz de Castro Neves, my father.

The week Tony is supposed to testify, we cannot get ahold of him. He will not answer any phone calls and we begin to worry. The night before he is to be called, his attorney calls my attorney and says Tony cannot testify. He is in the middle of a divorce and is having some problems.

It marks a low point in the trial for me—I feel deserted and disheartened.

But it is a moment when I find out who my friends really are—the people who continue to call, text, and e-mail all remind me that I am not alone. I receive far less messages than when I won Indy or when I was on *Dancing with the Stars,* but I am forever thankful for the people who stand by me.

On the morning of April 2, my friend Mark takes the stand. Matt Axelrod asks Mark why he refused to meet with the prosecutors to discuss the case. "The government asked on multiple occasions to see whether you would be willing to talk to us, right?"

"Yes," Mark says.

"And you refused to meet with us, didn't you?"

"I did. Do you want to know why?"

"Mr. Seiden, you're an experienced attorney, right?"

"Yes."

"You know how this works; I ask the questions, you give the answers."

"And I get to explain them if I want to."

"No."

The judge speaks up. "One moment. One moment. One moment. If he wants to explain an answer that you asked, he may."

"Yes, Your Honor. I think the question was just whether he refused to meet with us."

"But he wanted to explain his answer. And he may."

"Yes, Your Honor. Go ahead, Mr. Seiden."

"I didn't want to meet with you because you are unfairly prosecuting an innocent person, and I don't want to assist you in that endeavor."

Axelrod fumbles to get his words.

The court is silent. I feel as though we have just gained a few car lengths.

Mark goes on to explain the day of the Penske signing, the 2004 trial with Emerson, and the fact that this whole trial is ridiculous and should never have been brought before a federal court.

That afternoon, Americo Teixeira takes the stand. Americo has known my family and me since the start of my career. He is the editor of *Motorsports Brazil,* the official magazine for Brazilian Car Racing. He explains the intricacies of racing in Brazil, from go-karts up through Formula Three. He tells of when he first met my father and me in 1987 and how my father has always provided the support for me to race.

"I wanted to ask you about the years between 1999 and 2006," Roy says. "Were you aware of Helio Sr. publicizing Helio Jr.'s career, or talking to any journalists during those years?"

There is a pause as the translator tells Americo what Roy has just said. I flash back to the nightmare of the 2004 trial, when I took the stand and fumbled over the translation and the confusing line of questioning. I feel for Americo, but he answers with complete assurance.

"Yes, Helio, the father, was always the manager of Helio, the son's, career. He was not only in charge of several professional activities—he was also the main contact for the press."

"Would it be fair to say that Helio Sr. did a lot to promote the career and image of his son?"

"Helio Jr. would not have been the world champion, world idol, so to speak, without the support of his family. More specifically, the support of his father."

Americo's testimony is brilliant and starts to get emotional. As I listen to him, I get a bit teary-eyed. He holds up a photograph from 1989. "This is the year that—this is the win—I'm sorry." He chokes up a little. "This is the win that was conquered by Helio in 1989 for the Brazilian Championship." He begins to cry.

I feel a lump forming in the back of my throat.

"I'm sorry. I'm sorry," he says. "But to see this article, it reminds me of a very important moment . . . I'm sorry." He chokes up again.

I begin to sob. The attorneys ask for a recess. I go to the bathroom and Bob Bennett is there. He gives me a hug and as he embraces me, I try to calm myself. "Helio," he says, "I am from D.C. We don't hug many men in the bathroom, so this is a first for me." We start to laugh and I am able to pull myself back together again. I am ready to go back into the courtroom for the cross-examination of Americo.

Axelrod approaches the jury stand.

"My name is Matt Axelrod. I'm the assistant United States attorney, representing the United States in this matter. I have just a few questions for you, sir. It's apparent you are very close to the Castroneves family, aren't you?"

"Yes, I am."

"And your relationship with the Castroneves family goes back more than twenty years?"

"It's true. More than twenty years."

"And you care a lot about them?"

"A lot. I care a lot about them," Americo says.

"And you want to help them."

"I am here to tell the truth. If the truth will help them, it will be my pleasure."

"Because you care about them?"

"I care about truth and justice."

Again Axelrod fumbles. Again the court falls silent.

Okay, that's a few more car lengths, maybe a lap ahead.

ſ

The following day, it is my father's turn. This is the worst part of the whole trial for me. I knew it would be. I told my attorneys to let me testify instead of my dad, but funnily enough, I don't know enough about my own finances to take the stand. Also, it would be easy for the prosecutors to trick me, as that is what happened when I testified in the 2004 trial against Emerson. On any other day, my father is a teddy bear, loving and huggable. But on the witness stand, he is a bear, fierce and protective.

He lays out the whole story for the court from beginning to end. How much money he spent each year, how he was in charge of my finances, how he had used Seven Promotions to protect my money, not to defraud anybody. It is agonizing to watch him up there, struggling to tell the story, but stumbling when the translator doesn't interpret the questions clearly. It is even worse when Axelrod cross-examines him. He speaks to my father in a demeaning tone, as though he is stupid and dishonest.

"Did you or did you not sign these papers?" he yells at him.

Axelrod is asking the questions in the most confusing way possible. The interpreter is having trouble translating them clearly. Kati and I keep whispering to Howard and Roy, "That's not what he said. The translation is confusing the meaning!"

During the breaks, my father asks me, "How am I doing?"

"I don't know, Dad," I say as I fight back tears.

The judge lets us go for the day and informs the court that tomorrow we will hear the closing arguments. My stomach knots up when I hear him say that. I am happy this is coming to an end, but I am anxious about the verdict. As we leave the courtroom, Howard tells Kati and me, "Tonight is the first night of Passover. I would like you to come to our seder. You are a part of my family now."

At sundown, we arrive at Howard's for our first seder. His family embraces us immediately. "Come in! Come in! We are so glad you could make it." On a night when we should feel trepidation and fear, we only feel love and kindness. We are surrounded by at least thirty people, who tell us, all at once, "Sit, sit. Make yourselves at home."

We take our places at the end of a long table that has been beautifully arranged with crystal and china. Everybody is talking with the comfort and ease of people who have known each other forever. It makes me ache for my family and friends back home in Brazil—the people who knew me when I was a child. The people who know me as Helio, the person. Not Helio Castroneves the race car driver, or the guy who won *Dancing with the Stars*, or the guy on trial for tax evasion.

A seven-year-old boy limps to the front of the table to recite the four questions, which I learn is the custom in the Jewish religion. He has pale skin and thinning hair. He is small for his age. It is Luke, Howard's nephew, who has been battling cancer since he was three.

"Why is it that on all other nights during the year, we eat either bread or matzoh, but on this night we eat only matzoh?" Luke asks.

"Why is it that on all other nights we eat all kinds of herbs, but on this night we eat only bitter herbs?

"Why is it that on all other nights we don't dip our herbs even once, but on this night we dip them twice?

"Why is it that on all other nights we eat either sitting or reclining, but on this night we eat in the reclining position?"

Luke returns to his seat and I offer him a high-five. "Way to go, buddy. That was really great."

We get to talking and I relate to him better than I do to most adults. He sees me as just another regular guy. He is too young to know who I am or what I do—too pure to care.

I instinctively ask him, as I do all kids, "Hey, Luke, what do you want to be when you grow up?" Oh shit. As soon as the words slip out of my mouth I realize that this family worries if this boy will even reach adulthood. Here is a child whose very existence is in question.

"A professional basketball player. Maybe a soccer player. I haven't decided yet." The adults at the table are silent, all too aware that those are awfully big dreams for a child who has just gone through his third round of chemo. But he displays a refreshing level of optimism and courage, as only a child can. He believes that he can achieve anything, despite the fact that he is fighting a cancer I cannot even pronounce.

"Rhabdomyosarcoma," he tells me matter-of-factly.

Well, doesn't that just put everything in perspective?

Howard raises a plate of matzoh.

"This is the bread of affliction that our fathers ate in the land of Egypt. Whoever is hungry, let him come and eat; whoever is in need, let him come and conduct the seder of Passover. This year we are here; next year in the land of Israel. This year we are slaves; next year we will be free people."

"Why doesn't anyone ask why God made slaves of the Jews in the first place?" Howard asks the table. "Why aren't we questioning that, instead of thanking him for setting them free?"

When he sits back down, I whisper to him, "Because, my man, God has a plan."

CHAPTER 15

Closing In

**Begin at the beginning and go on until
you come to the end, then stop.**

—LEWIS CARROLL

I ENTER THE COURTROOM for the final push. I walk with my head up, confident in my innocence, and with full faith in God and the American justice system.

The white flag is waved—one lap to go. The closing statements.

The government starts off first and I brace myself for a rough beginning. At the onset, Axelrod tells the jury that there was no problem with sending the money to my father, even if he was in Brazil. It happens all the time. "Sending the money is admirable," he says, but deducting the money off your taxes, claiming you get a business deduction, claiming you should get a tax deduction for services that aren't being performed—that is not admirable. That is tax fraud. I want to scream at him. How many times do you have to hear about the money my father invested in my career? About all of the work that he did for me? How many times does it have to be stated that this was a business? This was not a Little League team. I know that he is just doing his job, but it makes my blood boil all the same. His statement goes on for four hours and I try not to listen. I cannot bear hearing him call me a criminal one more time.

∫

Then David presents all of the tax details. He explains once again that the money was sent to my father to pay him back for the millions of dollars he invested in my career. He explains once again why Alan sent my money to Fintage so that I would have a retirement fund for when I could no longer race. I fade in and out. I am so sick of hearing about constructive receipts and deferred payments. But this time I understand a bit more of what these terms mean. I look to the jury and hope that they do, too. It took me ten years to finally figure it out—would they be able to grasp the concept in six weeks? God, I hope so. I am too nervous to pay attention any longer. I finger the beads of my rosary and begin to pray. *Ave Maria, cheia de graca . . .*

We break for lunch. I cannot eat. I go with my family to the church across from the courthouse. We sit in silent prayer. We hardly speak. We are eager to get back to the courtroom and put the day behind us. Media members surround the courthouse and I am careful to keep a strong face as we walk through the crowd, back into the courthouse for our side's closing statements.

ſ

Bob Bennett stands in front of the jury, all 240 pounds of him, and he begins to deliver his closing. I pay attention. There is no way not to pay attention when Bob speaks.

"Good morning, ladies and gentlemen. My brothers and sisters at the bar. This was a very unfair indictment and presentation of the evidence. The prosecution took a vacuum cleaner approach to this case and they moved it around here and Brazil and elsewhere and then they took the contents and basically just dumped it in the jury box and are hoping that you, when you deliberate, will go back and try to put the pieces together and find a violation. This case was not only complex and confusing by the subject matter, but it was complex and confusing by the prosecution's presentation of the evidence.

"Just imagine a house of dirty, dirty windows: Even the most beautiful Florida day is going to look bad through those dirty windows. And that's what the government has done with this case, from the investigation to the prosecution. They are looking at everything through dirty windows. . . .

"There is a great British author by the name of Lewis Carroll, and he wrote these fabulous stories about a girl named Alice in Wonderland. And it seems that one day, Alice is walking in the woods and she falls down a rabbit hole. She goes down, down, down, down, and when she lands, she's on her feet and all of the Lewis Carroll colorful characters are there. There's the Mad Hatter, which is this gigantic rabbit with ears, you know, and a top hat. There's a frog with glasses. There's a goldfish bowl that has a goldfish in it. Except there's one thing that Alice notices: Everybody is upside down except her, and they look at her like there's something wrong with her. Well, ladies and gentlemen, I think my prosecutor friends fell down that rabbit hole. . . ."

Now he has everyone's attention. And he begins to take all of the facts of the case, pull them out of that rabbit hole, turn them right side up, and place them in the proper order. To clean the dirty windows. Everything begins to make sense.

"Do you think that when Kati and Helio signed that agreement, did they put their champagne glasses down and say, 'Time out, we have some business, Alan; please come into the bedroom and we'd like to invite you into our conspiracy to defraud the United States government'? And Alan Miller says, 'You look like two nice, lovely kids. I've lived sixty-one years of my life as an honorable man. Sure I'll join you in your criminal conspiracy to defraud the United States government.' It's preposterous, ladies and gentlemen. It's them looking through these dirty windows."

He ends with one last contemplation: "Ladies and gentlemen of the jury, my closing thought to you is this one. Think of this: When this case is over, after you have returned your verdict, you're going to go home to all the joys of your life. Judge Graham, he's going to go on to his next case. Mr. Dwyer and Mr. Axelrod will prosecute someone else. All of us defense lawyers will go on to our next cases. But Helio, Kati, and Alan will live with your verdict and their families will live with your verdict for the rest of their lives. We feel comfortable with it in your hands and I respectfully submit to you that the only fair verdict in this case is a verdict of not guilty to all defendants. Many thanks."

Roy steps up to the plate. It is like watching Ty Cobb follow Babe Ruth; or for those of us who did not grow up on baseball, it is like Pelé passing the soccer ball to Ronaldo. Roy explains once more that my money had been placed in Fintage as a retirement plan, not to defraud the U.S. government. And that Seven Promotions had been used so I could pay my father back for all he had done for me, again, not to defraud the U.S. government.

"And what did this man, Helio Sr., do for his son? He may have been obsessed, but think about what he did. He took a boy who was driving a car, who couldn't even get a name on it; it was there with a question mark instead of a sponsor's logo. He is almost at an end, is running out of money, he'd done an incredible job doing everything he can to support his son, and less than ten years later, through his efforts, this boy from a small town in Brazil goes from go-karts and a car without a name on it to being on top of the world, two times in a row winning in the Indianapolis 500 and missing the third time by a couple of thousandths of a second. That's what this man did for his son. He sacrificed everything. Sold all his property.

Bankrupted his company. Spent day and night working with him. Every weekend working with this young boy to become this man, this champion, this star on top of the world. How much is that worth? Can we even put a number on it? I don't know that we can. But I have to tell you, though it is hard to put a number on this, is there anybody who can say it is a crime to repay this man for what he did?"

I look to my father. My heart heaves for him. I wonder, when I have children, will I do what my father has done for me? Will I be that selfless? Will I be able to sacrifice everything for them? Will I be able to gamble my family's future in pursuit of one child's gift?

Roy continues: "As long as we are talking about fairness, let's talk about fairness to Helio for a second. He is a nonimmigrant person. He has an '01 visa, which means he stays here as long as he is driving and no longer. And what benefits does he get? What benefits does he get that all the rest of us get from paying taxes? He gets no Social Security, he gets no Medicare. You think when he goes back to Ribeirão Preto and takes his Medicare card to the local drugstore, they're going to give him his prescriptions or his doctor is going to treat him on that? Is that fair? He doesn't get any education here. He doesn't get permanent residency. He doesn't get citizenship. He doesn't have the right to vote. He has to ask for permission to travel. To get a mortgage, he has to put down thirty to forty percent. He has to renew his visa every three months. And guess what. The immigration service can throw him out whenever they want.

"And what happens if something happens to him? What happens if he is going two hundred fifty miles per hour and he hits another car or hits the wall and he's crippled or loses his legs or has brain damage? Who is going to take care of him?"

Just hearing this makes me anxious. These are the things that I never think about—I have trained myself to block out these realities. It is difficult and jarring to listen to Roy lay them out so baldly.

He goes on. "Because as soon as that happens, he's out of a job and he's out of this country. Who is going to take care of him? That's why they create funds like a retirement fund for people like this. Lawyers know this. Alan Miller knew this. This is why he sent five million dollars to Fintage, not to defraud the U.S. government, but to protect Helio."

It makes sense to me now. Alan had years of experience representing the best race car drivers in the world. I trusted my gut that he would do what was best for me, and he did. I signed a bunch of documents without reading them, and maybe that was my mistake. Maybe some people say I should have asked questions, instead of trusting others, but how was I to know all of the intricacies of the American tax code? I was a twenty-four-year-old race car driver from Brazil, just happy to have a ride. And even if I was a forty-five-year-old banker from New York, I doubt I would have understood that tax manual.

∫

Howard's summation takes us back to my family dinner table in 1987, when my father informed us that he had sold his property in Rio to hire Americo Teixeira as my publicist and to buy my racing equipment. "In some homes that might breed contempt," Howard explains. "In some homes that might breed sibling rivalry. But in Ribeirão Preto in 1987, when a father hired a public relations professional for an eleven-year-old boy, sister Kati understood. And she understood that it was not because they loved him more or because they favored him more, but she understood that the family was in a venture.

"The model in Ribeirão Preto in 1987, and 1988, and 1989, and 1990 was a sister devoting herself to the career of her brother, sacrificing herself for her brother, because she saw in him what her parents saw in him, what everyone else saw in him. . . ."

Howard goes on to tell of Kati's twenty-two years of dedication and conviction. I don't dare look over to her, for fear one of us will cry. I am doing okay until Howard starts to bring it home.

"Did Kati and Helio set out to come to this country to commit a crime? To not pay their taxes? Kati and Helio came to this country to pursue a dream. It was the dream of a father, the dream of a mother, the dream of a son, and the dream of a sister, a sister who dedicated herself to her brother selflessly, without jealousy, without envy, supporting her brother, without fame, indeed without fortune. She did it because she understood the purpose of this endeavor. She knew where it would end. She didn't think it would end in this courtroom, though . . ."

Hold on, I tell myself. Do not cry.

"She believed in her little brother, and she was there to support him throughout, to protect him. And that's what she's done."

I can feel the lump forming in my throat and my eyes begin to water.

"I thought of the movie, with two girls that grew up like sisters. One becomes a famous singer and the other living in her shadow. Bette Midler sang the song, you may recall it. The movie was *Beaches*: *"It must have been cold there in my shadow, / to never have sunlight on your face. / You were content to let me shine, that's your way. / You always walked a step behind."*

I hear sniffling all around me. I blink back the tears. I bite my lip.

The entire courtroom is in tears—the lawyers, the witnesses, even some of the jurors. The judge's law clerk quietly exits the courtroom so that no one will see that she, too, is weeping.

For a moment it feels like Kati and I are alone with Howard in the courtroom. No jury, no judge, no press, just a brother and sister coming to terms with a lifetime's worth of emotions. She has given everything of herself so that I could reach the top. Would I have done the same for her if she had needed me to give up my dream so that she could pursue hers?

I begin to cry, audibly. Kati is looking down, so I cannot see her face. I look at Howard and I can tell even he is choked up. I know that Kati and I are more than just clients to him. We have become family.

I look to Kati. Through her tears, she musters a smile.

It's going to be okay.

For the first time in a long time, I can smile back.

It's going to be okay.

∫

The feeling of warmth and security doesn't last long. The government presents a second closing. How many times do they get to go? I sit in silence and listen as the prosecutors once more call me what I am not—a criminal, a cheat, unethical, dishonorable. The blood rushes to my head. After what seems like an eternity, court is adjourned and the jury goes into deliberation. There is nothing to do but wait.

This proves to be the most agonizing part of the trial. I am certain of my innocence, but I am not certain what the jury is going to decide. Each morning, I wake up at five-thirty by force of habit. I wish I could sleep later to make the days go faster, but my body doesn't allow it. I go to church; then Kati and I drive to a friend's apartment near the courthouse. The judge has ordered that we stay no more than fifteen minutes away so when the verdict comes in, we can be there as quickly as possible. For the whole week we sit at the apartment waiting for a call.

No news is good news. I know that the longer the jury deliberates, the better our chances. The mornings are the worst. By the time two o'clock rolls around, we start to breathe easier. Maybe we will have one more night of peace? When the clock hits five we fully exhale. Everything is okay for a few hours. But the next day the torture begins again. Five-thirty in the morning. This goes on for a week.

I feel nothing. I have no control. I have given myself over to destiny. I will accept God's plan, whatever it may be.

On the seventh day, Kati and I decide we will await the verdict in the church across from the courthouse. The priest is leading a service in Spanish. He receives us for holy communion.

Y tomando el pan, habiendo dado gracias, partió, y les dio, diciendo:

Esto es mi cuerpo, que por vosotros es dado; haced esto en memoria de mí.

As we are walking down the aisle to return to our seats we spot Howard sitting in the last row of the church. For how long he has been there we don't know. He nods his head at us. *The jury has a verdict.*

Ave Maria, cheia de graca . . .

"Mr. Castroneves, stand up please." As soon as he says it, all of the emotions I have been holding in for the past six weeks begin to surge forth. I try to suppress them once again, but cannot hold on any longer. I stand up and then lose all control. I feel myself heaving and gulping for air. I am out of my body. I'm not sure how I am even standing. Muffled in the background, the judge begins to read my verdict. I cannot hear anything he says, just the echoes inside my own head, my gasps for breath.

All of a sudden, my attorney, David Garvin, grabs me, hugs me, and he repeats something to me over and over again until it becomes clear. "I told you it was going to be okay. I told you it was going to be okay." My senses slowly return to me and I hear the judge still speaking.

Kati grabs me and we hold each other.

There is a flurry of hugs and kisses, tears and laughter, and big, gasping sighs of relief. I am not yet sure that this is real.

Not guilty. Not guilty. I did not even hear Judge Graham say the words.

Once I am embraced in the arms of my family, I start to regain feeling and a sense of reality.

> *Well that was the silliest tea party I ever went to,*
> *I'm never going back there again!*
> —LEWIS CARROLL

CHAPTER 16

Back on Track

**Enthusiasm is everything.
It must be taut and vibrating,
like a guitar string.**

—PELÉ

THE NEXT MONTH plays out like a movie montage. My life comes at me in flashes instead of real time. It is all too much to process.

I go from the courtroom straight to an airplane bound for Long Beach, California. I step off the plane and see Cindric holding my helmet and my firesuit. I arrive at a racetrack where thousands of fans call out my name. I sit behind the wheel of my car and I take deep breaths. I have not been in a car in six months and it shows. I am trying to regain my groove, but during the qualifying round I spin out and crash. The race itself is truly a blur. I know that I finish in seventh, but I also know that for the first time in my life, I am not disappointed in seventh. I am just happy to be on the track.

For the next three weeks, I rent out an apartment in Indianapolis and set out to prepare for Indy. I realize that nobody expects me to win—I am months of practice behind everyone else. But I am determined to make up for lost time. Every day I am at the track from the minute it opens and until the minute it closes. Preparation for Indy is not just about practicing. I have to give an inordinate number of interviews, including several trips to New York for media appearances. For the weeks leading up to the race, I am barely sleeping. I am on airplanes, in race cars, going to late-night talk shows, and waking for early-morning practices. Not that I mind; I am thrilled to be awake all of the time. I finally feel like myself again, a race car driver chasing a checkered flag.

The world around me is still a bit foggy, a bit surreal. It is spinning too fast and my mind cannot keep up. And then the montage of practices and talk shows and interviews ends. Everything slows down and becomes very quiet. I realize that I am in familiar territory. I am standing on the starting line of the Indianapolis Motor Speedway with my hand to my heart, saluting the American flag.

ſ

The national anthem plays and four hundred thousand fans have their hands over their hearts. The final words echo through the stadium: ". . . o'er the land of the free, and the home of the brave."

Stand tall. Stay focused.

"Starting in the thirty-third position . . ."

"Starting in the tenth position . . ."

"Starting in the second position . . ."

"And starting in the pole position, two-time Indianapolis chaaampion, Helio Castroneves!"

The crowd goes wild. I can feel the butterflies. It is my favorite part of racing—the butterflies, the excitement and the nerves. I puff out my chest.

To be a champion, you must act like a champion.

The marching band begins to play "Back Home Again in Indiana." A thousand balloons are released into the sky.

Hang tough, I tell myself. Maintain control.

"Ladies and gentlemen, start your engines."

God has a plan. *Deus tem um plano.*

The flag drops and I am off. I know what I am here to do.

ſ

I am strapped into the race car, sweat dripping down the sides of my face; my heart is pumping. I feel the hum of the car. Four hundred thousand people fill the Indianapolis grandstand. I am calm and relaxed. I am home.

It is a five-hundred-mile race and it goes by in a heartbeat.

Until those final five laps.

I glance at the giant monitor and I see my name at the top of the leaderboard. I am leading by two seconds.

An image of Adri, Kati, my father, and my mother flashes on the screen. They are standing on a platform, gripping each other's hands. I know that they are anxious and uncertain. But I also know that the race is mine.

For the next five laps, I grip the steering wheel and do what I have been trained to do all my life.

At each corner, the adrenaline pumps even harder.

Three laps to go.

Look ahead.

Two laps to go.

Go faster.

The last lap.

Just drive.

I turn into the final straightaway. I don't look in my rearview mirror. I don't have to—I know that I have won.

As I cross the finish line, the world goes quiet and still for one sweet second.

And then it explodes.

Track officials run toward me. A massive crowd roars, drowning out any other sound but the voice in my head.

This is real. This is real.

I am crying. I am laughing. I am pumping my fists in the air. As the car slows to a stop, all I want to do is break free. I unbuckle myself and the track officials try to stop me from getting out of the car. But I jump out anyway. I run across the track and leap up on the fence. As I climb, I see a thousand Brazilian flags waving. I hear half a million people screaming my name.

For the first time in a long time, the world is broadcasting in high definition and surround sound.

I look out into the crowd of screaming fans and I take deep breaths.

I am back.

I look to the sky and everything goes quiet.

Deus tem um plano.

God has a plan.

The Beginning

DECEMBER 28, 2009. Five-thirty a.m. It is a cold Atlanta morning. The car thermometer reads thirty-one degrees. And I am sweating. Adriana and I are on our way to the hospital. In a matter of hours we will be parents. Adriana is cool and calm, as always, while I am nervous and excited.

Once we are at the hospital, the nurse admits us our room. Everyone is buzzing around Adriana, hooking her up to the monitor, taking her blood pressure, making her comfortable.

I am not sure what I should do, so I sit next to her and hold on to her leg, and wait. I am mesmerized by the movement on the screen and calmed by the low hum of the monitor.

A million thoughts are running through my head. Will I be as good a father as my dad? Will I be able to change her diapers the right way? Will we be able to raise her the way my parents have raised me?

From the start, I have been very lucky. I know that. Lucky to have a father who infected me with the racing obsession and was crazy enough to support me in my climb to the top. Lucky to have a mother who instilled a strong faith in me and was self-less enough to support my dreams no matter how nervous they made her. Lucky to have a sister who stuck by my side and was there to back me up every step of the way. They have helped to shape me into the man I am today. I have depended on them for the past thirty-five years of my life, sometimes perhaps a little too much. I did not want to leave the nest. It was comfortable and safe. I was content to be a son and a brother, protected and supported by my parents and sister.

But today is the day I become a father.

Somebody is going to turn to me for help for the next thirty-five years. I only hope that I can be as selfless as my parents have been with me. I pray that I can inspire my daughter to follow her dreams and then be there for her when she needs me to help her achieve them. I will repeat to her the same philosophies I was raised by: "To be a champion, you must act like a champion." And "God has a plan."

And one day, when she still feels like listening to me, I will sit her down and tell her who I was before she came along and changed my life.

I was a race car driver, an Indy 500 champion; I won a dance competition. I may even show her the video as proof. I was a guy who was born lucky, rose to the top, then quickly fell to the bottom before rising back up again. Then, only a few months before she was born, I almost fell back down the rabbit hole in a trial defending myself against the U.S. government. I will tell her all of this, but first I will tell her about the day I found out she was on her way.

We were at a racetrack, of course. It was a few days before the 2009 Indianapolis 500. "I have something to tell you," her mother said. And before Adriana uttered the words, I knew. I started to laugh, cry, and jump around. If all of life is a race, this was the day God guided me back on track.

Take the wheel, He said, *and go forward. This is the first day of the rest of your life.*

For months, a federal trial forced me to look back, something I had not done in all my life. Racing had trained me to keep my focus straight ahead. Don't dwell, don't fret, it will not get you anywhere, I was told. And for the most part this was true. But I learned the value in looking in the rearview mirror from time to time. I discovered who I was, and I learned to anticipate who I wanted to become. I came to cherish the beautiful ups and downs that God has thrown at me—Indy wins, family bankruptcy, *Dancing with the Stars*, a federal indictment, and now fatherhood.

By looking back, I have developed a more clear focus on the future. I tell myself what I will someday tell my daughter.

Take each day as it comes. Every challenge should be met in its own time. All of life is a race. You are not going to win it in the first lap. You have to pace yourself, save fuel, hang in there when it gets a little scary. Sometimes you have to change your strategy. Sometimes you have to go maximum speed. Don't forget, it is a team effort— you are not alone, though it may feel like it at times. Maintain control. Trust yourself when all others doubt you. Remember, if there is a problem, it is because there is a solution for it.

ſ

At 4:15, Mikaella is born. When she comes into the world, all is quiet. Then the doctor slaps her and she begins to cry. It

is the most beautiful sound I have ever heard. My heart feels like it is going to come out of my chest. I cannot stop looking at her. I cannot stop smiling, crying, laughing. I realize that this is the greatest moment that I will ever know.

Minutes later, the nurse hands me my beautiful baby girl. Everything about her amazes me. Her perfect eyes, her perfect hands, her perfect lips, her full head of hair. It takes me a minute to catch my breath.

I feel her heart beating against mine and my world shifts. *Thank you, God, for this beautiful plan.*

The race is long and in the end, it's only with yourself.

Appendix

INDYCAR SERIES HIGHLIGHTS

First start: March 18, 2001 (Phoenix International Raceway)

First victory: May 27, 2001 (Indianapolis Motor Speedway)

First pole: March 17, 2002 (Phoenix International Raceway)

2009

- Finished fourth in the IndyCar Series standings for Team Penske with two victories and one earned pole position.
- Won pole for the ninety-third Indianapolis 500.
- Won his third Indianapolis 500, becoming only the fourth driver to win three times at Indianapolis and the first to do so since Al Unser in 1970–71.

2008

- Finished second in the IndyCar Series standings for Team Penske with two victories and three earned pole positions, bringing career total to thirty-three earned poles.
- Extended his record of consecutive years with a win to nine.

2007

- Finished sixth in IndyCar Series standings for Team Penske with victory at St. Petersburg, Florida.
- Recorded six top-five and eleven top-ten finishes.
- Won pole for the ninety-first Indianapolis 500.
- Set IndyCar Series record with seven poles (St. Petersburg, Motegi, Indianapolis, Milwaukee, Watkins Glen, Mid-Ohio and Belle Isle).

2006

- Finished third in IndyCar Series standings for Team Penske with four victories and five earned pole positions.
- Won at St. Petersburg, Motegi, Texas, and Michigan.
- Recorded nine top-five and twelve top-ten finishes.
- Won consecutive pole positions at Milwaukee, Michigan, and Kentucky and earned pole positions at Watkins Glen and Richmond based on practice speed.
- Also started on pole at Motegi, when lineup was set by points.

2005

- Finished sixth in IndyCar Series standings for Team Penske with victory at Richmond International Raceway.
- Recorded eight top-five and eleven top-ten finishes.
- Led eight races for 230 laps.
- Earned pole positions at Pikes Peak and Watkins Glen.

2004

- Finished fourth in IndyCar Series standings with a victory at Texas2. Scored six top-five finishes and thirteen top-ten finishes.
- Earned five MBNA Pole Awards (Richmond, Nazareth, Chicagoland, California, Texas2) and tied Billy Boat's 1998 record of four consecutive pole victories.

2003

- Finished third in IndyCar Series standings with race victories at Gateway and Nazareth. Scored nine top-five finishes, tying him with three other drivers for most top fives.
- Earned three pole positions (Indianapolis, Gateway, California) and eleven top-ten finishes.
- Captured MBNA Pole for eighty-seventh Indianapolis 500, becoming the first back-to-back 500 winner to win the pole for his attempt to win three in a row. Finished second in the race, making his results of first, first, second in his first three starts at Indianapolis the best of any driver in 500 history.

2002

- Won second consecutive Indianapolis 500 in Marlboro Team Penske entry, becoming the fifth driver to win consecutive races at Indianapolis and the first to do so since Al Unser in 1970–71. First driver in Indianapolis 500 history to win race in each of his first two starts.
- Finished second in point standings in first full season of IndyCar Series competition, scoring wins at Indianapolis and Phoenix. Won MBNA Pole at Phoenix. Scored seven top-three finishes, twelve top-five finishes, and fourteen top-ten finishes.

2001

- Won Indianapolis 500 by 1.7373 seconds over Marlboro Team Penske teammate Gil de Ferran. Led final fifty-two laps after starting eleventh.
- Delivered eleventh Indianapolis 500 victory to team owner Roger Penske.
- Started seventeenth, finished eighteenth at Phoenix in only other IndyCar Series start.

ROAD TO INDYCAR SERIES

2001

- Finished career-best fourth in CART standings with Marlboro Team Penske, winning from the pole at Long Beach and Detroit. Also won race at Mid-Ohio and pole at Motegi.

2000

- Earned three victories (Detroit, Mid-Ohio, Laguna Seca) and three poles and finished seventh in CART point standings in first year with Marlboro Team Penske.
- First career CART victory came at Detroit.

1999

- Finished fifteenth in CART point standings in first season with Hogan Racing.
- Earned first career pole at Milwaukee.

1998

- Finished second in CART Rookie of the Year standings driving for Bettenhausen Motorsports.
- Led thirty-seven laps, best among rookies.

1997

- Finished second in the PPG-Dayton Indy Lights championship by four points.

- Earned Indy Lights victories at Long Beach, Savannah, and Toronto. Won four Indy Lights pole positions.

1996

- Finished seventh in first Indy Lights season driving for Tasman Motorsports.
- Earned first career Indy Lights victory from the pole at Trois-Rivières.

1995

- Finished third in British Formula Three championship driving for Paul Stewart Racing with victory at Donington Park.

1994

- Finished second in the Brazilian Formula Three championship with four victories. Recorded four poles.
- Raced in British Formula Three series.

1993

- Finished second in South American Formula Three championship with four wins and three poles.

1992

- Finished second in Brazilian Formula Vauxhall championship.

EARLY CAREER

- Competed in kart racing, winning a Brazilian national title and racing in the World Cup go-kart championship in Europe.

Acknowledgments

I WOULD LIKE to thank all of those who have played a part in my achievement:

Starting with the Castroneves Racing Family: Fernanda, my assistant—for keeping my life in order. Edu, my brother-in-law, and the greatest Web site administrator. In Brazil, Jack McMann, Jurandir, and Aleteia, you have been there for me since the beginning.

My uncle Cicero, my aunt Mara, my cousins Cicinho, Anelise, and Fernanda, who have all been in the stands since my first go-kart days, videotaping the races and cheering me on.

My aunt Sheila, grandmother Cely, cousin Leonardo— you were also there from the beginning, helping to keep my mom calm on the sidelines.

Also Uncle Xani, cousins Xaninho, Ricardo, Aline—even though you lived farther away, you were always supporting me in thought and prayer.

My grandpa and grandma, Diniz and Elza, though you are no longer here, I am sure you are still looking over me.

My cousins from Brasilia, Luis Paulo and Elaine, and their children, Dimitrius, Ludmila, Raissa—who always gave me a place to stay in Brasilia and always came to my races.

My friends from school: Guillherme Lepore, who today is

the *padrinho* of my daughter. Also Roger, Bola (Daniel but for me always Bola), Miguel, Saulo, Carlao, Lesura, Daniel Branco, Marcelinho, Matheus, Marina Salles, Bim, and the school's Marista, Objetivo.

My Corpal Team: Edu, Rubao, Ariovaldo, Tío Guaraná, Joao, Mane, Tato and Passoca plus Pedro Mulfato and Lagarto. Without you guys I would never be where I am today.

Team Nasr: Amir, Samir, Munir, Carlao, Luigi, Andre, and many others. I'll never forget the great time we had together.

The friends I made when racing in the United Kingdom, including Paul Stewart and Sir Jackie, who remain great friends today, as well as Vince Howard.

My first team in America, Tasman Motorsports, Steve and Christy Horne—thank you for believing in me, against all odds. Your support was invaluable.

Tony Bettenhausen and Carl Hogan. Though you are no longer here, you are certainly very much in my heart.

Roger and Kathy Penske and the entire Penske family. Thank you for the kindness you have shown me over the years. You have always made me feel part of your family.

All of my friends at Penske Corporation, especially Walter Czarnecki and Bud Denker. Thank you for all of your support.

Tim Cindric, my master strategist. I could never do it without you. And thanks for always understanding my English.

Everyone at Team Penske. Thanks for always being behind me through thick and thin. I am proud to be your teammate. Troy Anderson, Randy Ankeny, Noel Arnold, Bob Berlin, Andy Borme, Mike Brown, Joe Giordano, Brian Goble, Keith Goslin, Sean Hanrahan, Tim Harris, John Haslett, J. T. Horn, Eric Horsfield, Clive Howell, Pat Hozza, Trevor Jackson, Tim Lambert, Scott Leitheiser, Damon Lopez, Geoff Miller, Grant Newbury, Corey Odenbrett, John Piccinotti, Eric Prentice, Mike Ribas, Rick Rinaman, James Rosemond, Matt Rosentel, Ron Ruzewski, Chris Schwartz, Scott Shimp, Joshua Sides, Tim White, Aaron Yaeger, and Gary Yingst.

Four-time Indianapolis 500 winner Rick Mears, the Oval Master himself, for everything he taught me about winning at the Indianapolis Motor Speedway.

The teammates who made me better: Gil de Ferran, Sam Hornish, Jr., Ryan Briscoe, and Will Power. And the competitors who constantly challenge me.

My first trainer, Silviano Domingues, who put me on the right path all those years ago in São Paulo gym. And my current trainer, Carlos Bailey, who thinks he can kick my butt, but of course he can't. Hehe.

My PR team, which was always there behind the scenes making sense of what I was saying—Susan Bradshaw, Lisa Boggs, Jeremy Riffle, Adam Hoover, Dan Passe, Merrill Cain, and the master of all PR—Dan Luginbuhl, or DRL.

The *Dancing with the Stars* family: Deena Katz, Julianne Hough, Amy Astley, the entire cast and crew, and Apolo Ohno for getting me involved in the first place.

The legal team that won my case: David Garvin, Roy Black, Howard and Scotty Srebnick, Mark Seiden, Bob Bennett, Lilly Sanchez, David Leland, Alan Miller, Carlos Samlut, and Noah Fox. Thank you for believing in Kati and me and restoring our faith in the justice system.

The guys whom I became friends with during and after my trial: Michael Joseph, Ali Soltani, and Michael Fux.

My tennis and poker buddies in Miami: Kiko, Edson, Ronaldo, Sandrinho, Paulinho Rebenboi, Paulo Bachi, Flavio, Raul, Fernando Campos, Ricardo Echenike, Dante, and Oswaldo Negri.

The great guys from São Paulo who helped me in my early years: FHJ, Raul Seabra, Americo, Edu H. Mello, Familia Chiattone Alves, Andre Duek, Altair, Siciliano, Sucre, Dieter, Marina Lima, Fatima, Willie Herman, Carlo Gancia, Silviano, Gandini, Sergio Chamon, Jose Luis Balardini, Seu Mario and Mario Sergio, and Leandro (Lele).

My spiritual guides: Father Phil DeRea, Padre Mario, Padre Jaco, Lurdinha, Padre Primo, Bob Hills, and Don Ancelmo.

My wonderful editor, Ian Jackman, and my publisher, Raymond Garcia, and his team at Penguin, especially Kim Suarez.

My book writer, Marissa Matteo. Great job and thank you.

And of course, Adriana, Mikaella, Mom, Dad, Kati, Edu, and little Edu.

All the friends not mentioned here—the fans and acquaintances who cheer me on and send prayers and good wishes. Thank you!

Credits

Photos on pages xiii, 7, 81, 115, 129, 145, 199, 223, 253, 271, and 275: Courtesy of the author.

Photo on pages 2–3: IMS photo by Dan Helrigel.

Photos on pages 23, 63, 157, and 211: Photography by Miguel Costa Jr.

Photo on page 171: Carol Kaelson/Disney ABC Television Group/ABC via Getty Images.

Photo on page 235: *El Nuevo Herald,* 2009.

Photo on page 265: IMS photo by Jim Haines.